PSYCHICAL AND SPIRITUAL

Parapsychology in Christian faith and life

by

Michael Perry

CFPSS

First printed 2003

ISBN 0 902666 43 6

© Michael Charles Perry 2003

Published by
The Churches' Fellowship for Psychical and Spiritual Studies
The Rural Workshop, South Road, North Somercotes
Louth, Lincolnshire LN11 7PT

Printed in Great Britain by
The City Printing Works (Chester-le-Street) Ltd

CONTENTS

Foreword v

1 A parapsychological pilgrimage 1
2 'What a piece of work is a man!' 23
3 The Bible tells me so 48
4 From the realms of glory 71
5 Post-mortem prospects 95
6 Christian parapsychology................. 122

Index 149

Foreword

In 1978, the Churches' Fellowship for Psychical and Spiritual Studies (the CFPSS) asked me to be the editor of its theological quarterly THE CHRISTIAN PARAPSYCHOLOGIST. In the twenty-five years since then, I have had the immense privilege of working with a great host of creative thinkers on the boundaries between psychical research and Christian theology. As the Fellowship approached its fiftieth anniversary, I wanted to be able to set down what I believe, and where I have got to, in my own exploration of a subject which has exercised a lifetime's fascination, and to show how it has enriched both my devotion to Jesus Christ and my understanding of the Christian faith.

The subject is vast, and given the time, the will, and the mental energy, I would have had no difficulty at all in expanding every chapter of what follows into a volume on its own - indeed, in some cases, several volumes. But I wanted to write a book, not a library. It seemed to me that there would be something to be said for a modest, non-technical, work which would present the evidence as accessibly as possible without overburdening the text with references and footnotes. For those who wish to pursue the subject further there are many, and more specialised, publications.

Any permanent value there may be in the following pages owes an immense debt to the many members of the Fellowship and contributors to THE CHRISTIAN PARAPSYCHOLOGIST with whom I have engaged over the years. In particular, I must thank Andrew Beaizley, Julian Drewett, and particularly Neil Broadbent, for their kindly but critical comments on drafts of this book as they appeared, and Elizabeth Bowen and Julian Drewett for their meticulous proof-reading. For the final form, however, none but I can assume responsibility. It may, like Touchstone's Audrey, be an ill-favoured thing, but it is mine own. It is offered in the hopes that it may lead to increased understanding between those whose approach to the mysteries of creation are mainly psychical and those for whom the spiritual takes precedence.

Michael Perry
Durham

1

A parapsychological pilgrimage

When I was at primary school, I became fascinated by chemistry. It was all because of my cousin. He was five years older than me, and he taught me how to make gunpowder. He also told me that if I passed the scholarship and got to the Grammar School, *I* would be able to learn how to make even more powerful explosives.

So I got to the Grammar School, and began to learn about chemistry. By the time I reached the Sixth Form, it was the late 1940s and the whole of science seemed to me to be a world of the most exciting possibilities. We lived out in the sticks. It was ten miles to the nearest bookshop (and twenty to the nearest *good* bookshop), but every time I went to the Midland Educational at Leicester I would look out for the latest blue-backed Pelican book on a scientific subject and devour it with the greatest enthusiasm.

We had a school Scientific Society. One of the chores for the members of the Upper Sixth was that each of us had to give a talk to it at least once during our time. When my turn came round, I had just discovered a Pelican book by G.N.M. Tyrrell. It was called *The Personality of Man* and subtitled *New Facts and their Significance*. My copy (like me, it is now getting brown with age and a bit dog-eared at the corners) is the 1948 reprint of a book first published in 1947.

The new facts and their significance were about telepathy and foreknowledge, psychical research in the laboratory, mediumship, discarnate agency, and the physical phenomena of the séance room. And its final chapter was headed 'Psychical Research and Religion'.

I spoke to the Scientific Society about these new facts and their significance because, in my mid-teens, I had never heard about anything like this before. I had never come across the psychic dimension. I knew nothing of telepathy, clairvoyance, trances or mediums. But this whole area of study that Tyrrell was writing about opened up to me the most exciting vistas.

That was because I was *also* a keen and practising Christian - choir, Sunday School, Youth Fellowship; you name it, I was into it. I believed (of course I believed) in the resurrection of the body and the life of the world to come, but I knew that this was a matter of faith, a matter of trusting the Bible, and there certainly was no way (at least, not any way I knew) of finding out whether that faith was well-founded or not. I would have to wait till the very end of my life, and then, I presumed, I would discover (or not) whether it was all like I had been told, or whether I had been misinformed. For the time being, I had to accept what I had been told on authority. There were no facts (well, not any *scientific* facts) to go on. I had to live by faith.

And now here was a scientist telling me that new facts *had* been discovered. Scientific facts with a religious significance. What I had hitherto taken on trust as a believing Christian, could be proved by the application of scientific method and scientific procedures.

Are you surprised that I was excited? All of a sudden, the two disparate sides of my life, the chemistry and the Church, had clicked together and were seen to belong in one stereoscopic vision. Life would never be the same again.

That was more than fifty years ago, and it began what you might call a parapsychological pilgrimage which has lasted the rest of my life.

Fifty years ago, people were looking to science to solve all the problems of the world. I remember the incredulity of some of my parents' friends when they learned I was not going to pursue a career in science, but was seeking ordination. They could not understand why I was deserting a career with immense potential for improving the lives of the whole of mankind, so that I could spend the rest of my time drinking tea with old ladies.

Times have changed. Today, at the beginning of the twenty-first century, there may still be a feeling of excitement at the amazingly rapid advances of science and technology. We are only at the very beginning of the electronic era, and yet, even now, we can use our computers to gain access to information, and communicate with our friends at the other side of the globe, with an ease that we would never have dreamed of ten or twenty years ago. New and exciting discoveries are being made in science and medicine, almost by the day. The human genome has been mapped, and nobody knows what advances in medical treatment that is going to bring.

Yet there is also a feeling that scientific advance is careering forward faster than we can cope with it. It has led to problems (such as global pollution) which it doesn't seem capable of solving. It has treated the material world as though it were an infinite resource which could be plundered at will by a greedy humanity, instead of seeing the whole eco-system as a living whole which needs to be nurtured and respected for its own sake. We are beginning to realise that we need to see humanity as one part of an inter-dependent Nature, not as Nature's selfish tyrant.

Alongside this feeling that science has not found answers to the many problems that its advances have caused, there are signs of a new respect for religion and a widespread interest in the paranormal which would have seemed amazing in the mid-twentieth century.

Unfortunately, it is not a discriminating interest. The media never seem to tire of reporting parapsychological trivia. Every week there seem to be more programmes on television, and more articles in popular magazines, which make claims which far outstrip the evidence. What is true of parapsychology is also true of religion. Anyone who finds themselves on the mailing list of 'New Age' organisations soon realises that, as the twenty-first century gets going, there is an upsurge in spiritual hunger. Sadly, the response is often to offer junk food to the public, rather than anything which could be described as a nourishing spirituality.

It does not have to be like that. There is need for a discriminating look at the whole picture, to see what 'the psychic' really is, and how it can support and reinforce a mature spirituality.

That is why I have written this book. But let me begin with a disclaimer. I cannot write with any authority about 'religion' in general. I am a lifelong Christian, and I believe that the faith of the mainstream Christian churches is consistent with an interest in things psychic. It is from that standpoint alone that I can have anything worthwhile to say.

#

Fifty years ago, I believed that psychical research could be a real bridge between the religion in which I had been brought up and the science in which I found such fascination. It could provide proof for things which I had hitherto assumed could only be a matter of faith.

For instance, in Tyrrell's book I read that at the turn of the twentieth century, Frederic Myers, one of the founders of the Society for Psychical Research and a Fellow of Trinity College, Cambridge, had predicted that

> in consequence of the new evidence, all reasonable men, a century hence, will believe the Resurrection of Christ, whereas, in default of the new evidence, no reasonable men, a century hence, would have believed it. ... Veritable manifestations do reach us from beyond the grave. The central truth of Christianity is thus confirmed, as never before.

I went to a lecture in September 1953 on 'Psychic Research and the Resurrection'. With the arrogance of the twenty-year-old, I thought I could do better, and wrote an article on the same subject for an American journal called *Tomorrow*. Five years later, it became my first book - *The Easter Enigma*, sub-titled as 'an

A parapsychological pilgrimage

Essay on the Resurrection with special reference to the data of Psychical Research'.

That was about half-way through Frederic Myers' century. In hindsight, I do not think his prophecy about believing in the Resurrection was half true by then, and I certainly do not think it has become true even yet, at the end of that hundred years.

That is because, if psychical research is regarded as a bridge to link science and religion, it is a bridge which is not much used. Not very many people on the scientific side of it want to use it to come to religious truths, and even fewer on the religious side want to use it in order to have scientific verification of their beliefs. A lot of people believe it is a rickety structure and they are unwilling to trust themselves to it. But *some* bridge is needed. Scientists and religious thinkers need to engage with each other, and to incorporate the depths of each other's human experience into their own thinking. And a bridge is better than an island, which is the analogy one is forced to use about people who treat parapsychology and religion as ghettos standing over and against each other without mutual contact; and better than a pier, which wants to reach out but is still so rigidly defined as to be incapable of movement. A bridge, if it is properly constructed, can be secure enough to welcome people from either end. The Latin for bridge is *pons* and a bridge-builder is a *pontifex*. I would like to be a bridge-builder, but if I am to construct a psychic bridge between science and religion, the last thing I can do is to pontificate.

Why?

#

Part of the trouble lies with the way in which so many of the findings of academic parapsychology are expressed in statistical terms. They are not like the findings of our schoolday physics. Perhaps you remember learning about Boyle's Law? If you allow the temperature and the pressure of a mass of gas both to change at the same time, you can not discover any useful law which indicates how the volume changes. But if you keep the temperature constant and vary the pressure, you discover that its volume is proportional to the pressure. And if you keep the pressure constant, and vary the temperature, you discover that its volume is proportional to the absolute temperature. The physical scientists make their discoveries by isolating one particular variable and making sure that everything else in the experimental set-up remains constant. One variable at a time is the most they can deal with. The phrase my science teacher kept thumping at me was 'other things being equal, ...'.

That, of course, is all very well when you are dealing with a tube of hydrogen. Other things *can* be kept equal. But when you start dealing with human beings, the number of possible independent variables has become almost infinite, and you cannot isolate just one variable and see what happens to it when you carry out a particular experiment.

For example. How can you prove that if you take an aspirin every other day, it reduces your chance of having a heart attack? You cannot say that nobody who takes an aspirin ever has a heart attack. It is not as straightforward as that. Some people take aspirin regularly and still die of heart failure; and some people never take aspirin and yet they never have a heart attack. So what the researchers had to do was to take a sample population, give half of them an aspirin every other day, and half of them a tablet that looked like aspirin but was medically inert. After five years there had been 17 heart attacks per thousand in the men who had not taken the aspirin and 9 per thousand in those who had.

That sounds pretty conclusive - and so it is. Nearly twice the chance of a heart attack if you don't take aspirin. But all it is, is a statistical correlation, and statistics is an odd science. The researchers had used a sample of 22,000 individuals. If they had done the experiment with only 2000 subjects instead of 22,000, and had got precisely the same percentage results, the significance would have been nil, because it could just as well have happened by chance. In other words, you have to have a large enough sample if your statistics are to work.

Experiments with human beings are not like proving Boyle's

law. We have to be content with statistical correlations.

That is all well and good when you are talking about heart attacks and aspirin. People accept the statistical results of medical experiments like that. But when we talk about parapsychology, the scientists are not nearly so willing to accept the results of the statistics. There are many parapsychological experiments which have achieved much greater odds against chance than the experiment on aspirin and heart attacks. But the one with aspirin has become accepted mainstream medical science and the ones with telepathy are still controversial.

The difficulty is that the things which the parapsychologists are discovering go so much against the grain of what is the accepted norm in the mechanical sciences that it is easier to believe that something is going wrong with their experiments than that the whole of the theoretical basis of physical science needs re-thinking. A scientist does not throw aside the whole of his accustomed way of thinking about the world as the result of a single experiment, or even of a long series of experiments. Indeed, even the aspirin-and-heart-attack experiments have their critics, who say that the experimental protocol was faulty, so the results cannot be relied upon. The researchers only used male subjects, so there is no telling whether the effect would have been the same had there been females in the subject groups. And they used, not pure aspirin, but aspirin with a proportion of magnesium salts added to act as a buffer against its inherent acidity. How do we know that it was the aspirin rather than the magnesium salts which helped prevent the heart attacks? Scientists need to be very sure before they take new ideas on board. They can do so fairly easily with ideas like the effectiveness of certain drugs for certain conditions. But when it comes to more fundamental changes to the way they are being asked to think, it is by no means so simple. The way in which scientific thinking changes is a very subtle one.

Look how it came about with astronomy at the time of Copernicus, or with the laws of motion when Einstein put forward the theory of relativity. It was not that a single earth-shattering experiment took place and all the scientists in the world immediately changed their ideas about how the universe was put together. It was a slower and more hesitant story.

What happens is that we begin with a situation in which the old view satisfies everyone. Then, at odd spots or on odd occasions, there crop up new and troublesome data which just do not fit. But they do not immediately overthrow the existing order. At first, they are simply ignored. Perhaps they are artefacts of a badly-designed experimental set-up. Perhaps they are just errors in measurement. Perhaps they are the result of uncontrolled independent variables. Perhaps they will not crop up again when a different set of experimenters in another laboratory do the same experiment again. Perhaps they will just go away if we don't worry them.

And, often enough, they *do* go away. The history of science is littered with the débris of unexplained facts which have found no logical place in any overall view of the universe. It is simply impossible to recast the whole of science to fit one or two maverick observations. If we try to do so; if we bend the structure at that place; then it warps so much out of true in another place that we simply have to let it straighten itself out again. The attempt to fit it in has caused more anomalies than it solves. And we will always have to live with a residue of the unexplained. We just have to shrug our shoulders and get on with interpreting the 99.9% of our experience which fits comfortably within our existing scientific paradigm.

But then the awkward phenomena multiply, and the success rate of the existing theory begins to fall too far below the acceptable 99.9%. At first, the scientists just adjust the old theory to fit them in. That is what happened with the old theory of the universe which had the earth at the centre, and the sun and stars going round it in circular orbits. Astronomers began to find that the more accurate their observations, the less satisfactory the old theory was. So they 'saved the appearances' (as the saying went) by imagining that there had to be little orbits, or 'epicycles', superimposed on the main ones. When even this failed to work, and they had to have even smaller orbits super-superimposed on the little ones, the theory began to be more complicated than the data it was supposed to explain.

And then, a scientific genius made his great imaginative leap forward. There was a Copernican revolution. 'Let's see what happens', said Copernicus, 'if we put the sun at the centre, not the earth; and if we make the orbits elliptical instead of circular'. What an implausible idea! Everyone can see that the earth is at the centre, and, anyhow, the Bible says it is. But try it out on the data, and it works!

There was a period of intense confusion, when the old and the new theories were struggling for superiority. There were innumerable rearguard actions by people who could not see why the old ways could not be adapted a bit more and a bit longer. But in the end, the new theory won.

That is what happened with the Copernican revolution in astronomy. That is what happened with Einstein's revolution in physics. A new explanation was put forward; an explanation which allowed all the old facts to be true, but explained them in a different way which fitted the maverick facts in as well. Facts which do not fit into your system do not do anybody any good. You cannot ditch the whole system just because of them, *unless* you can find a new system which not only explains the old facts, but fits the new ones in as well. That is what happened with Newton and Einstein. Einstein did more than simply make sense of some strange facts about inter-stellar phenomena; he also explained the old mechanics in a new way which enabled him to fit both the old and the new into a single over-arching system.

Can the same sort of thing happen in respect of the evidence for telepathy? At present, we seem to be in the position of accumulating evidence which reduces the success rate of conventional scientific explanations below the critical 99.9%. That is not sufficient to make people change their whole view of the universe. Most people prefer simply to suspend their judgement on the experimental evidence. Though it has been steadily growing over at least the last sixty years, since the pioneering experiments of Dr Rhine, many people are not willing to accept it because they have an overall world-view which does not include it as a possibility. That world-view has taken them all their life-time to build up and to test against the available evidence, and it has held together in a way they found convincing. It is easier to dismiss the work of Rhine and his followers as no more than a few maverick observations, and they are not going to abandon their whole philosophy of life just because of *them*.

But what happens when the evidence continues to mount? The pressure to re-think one's scientific philosophy becomes more and more intense. For a while, one can file these odd facts in a kind of mental 'pending tray'. But in the end, for some people at least, there are just *too many* odd facts, and they have to admit that their old view of the world is just not good enough. They have to give in and believe that it is possible for mind-to-mind communication to take place. They have become converted to a belief in the reality of telepathy.

But they are still in a minority. And they are in the minority for two main reasons.

The first is that a parapsychological event is like a will-o'-the-wisp. It is occasional, evanescent, and totally unpredictable. Scientists like to conduct experiments of such a kind that any subsequent competent investigator can conduct them again and get the same result as the original experimenters. Parapsychology is still seeking the repeatable experiment. Currently, many hopes are pinned on experiments with the *Ganzfeld*, which seem to be more consistently repeatable, or the technique of *meta-analysis*, which pushes the statistical argument for paranormal activity to its absolute limits. What do these terms describe?

Ganzfeld is a German word meaning 'total field'. In a Ganzfeld experiment, a volunteer is put into a relaxed mood, lying on a comfortable couch, shielded as far as possible from all sensory input. His ears are covered by muffs and 'white' noise is fed in. This makes a swishing sound of many different frequencies so that nothing concrete is perceptible. Similarly, he is shielded from visual input by having halved ping-pong balls taped over the eyes. The purpose of the experiment is to see whether he can receive information which it would be impossible for him to pick up by the use of his normal senses. The target is usually a picture or drawing, and when it is displayed (often miles away from the receiver) the receiver records what he is thinking about, or visualising. Judges assess whether the receiver's thoughts are anything like the target picture or whether any similarities are simply coincidental and due to lucky guesswork. Results of Ganzfeld tests over the past years have been more consistent than in any other kind of parapsychological investigation.

In *meta-analysis*, the results of large numbers of experiments done by different investigators in different laboratories at different times are combined. Each individual experiment may be only marginally better than the result expected by pure chance, and critics could claim that for every experiment reported with a one-in-a-hundred probability of being a fluke, there must have been at least ninety-nine which were at chance significance and therefore were never reported. But when all experiments of a similar nature are combined in one analysis, it is like the aspirin statistics we saw a few pages back, only this time it works in the other direction. The 'chance' figure becomes such that it would need an astronomical number of unreported experiments to reduce the significance of the combined findings; and, since the analysis includes so many different experiments with so many different kinds of experimental set-up, it is harder for the sceptics to maintain that the result must be due to an undetected leakage of information or a sloppily designed experimental format.

Admittedly, the very fact that we have to depend on meta-analysis to help convince sceptics that the phenomena which parapsychologists are investigating do actually exist, shows the enormous disparity in scale between the size of effect with which the laboratory experimenter has to be satisfied and the kind of reported event which is alleged to occur in the world outside. For example, in a typical experiment in psycho-kinesis during the Rhine era, the experimenters would ask a subject to will that the dice should fall in a certain way. Sometimes it worked, but it could only be shown to be significant by the use of quite sophisticated statistics. Compare that with a typical account of the goings-on in a house afflicted by poltergeist activity, and we begin to wonder whether the things which have been reported in the outside world could ever have happened. (Perhaps they didn't? Or perhaps the laboratory researchers are like people investigating the electric power of a thunderstorm by working on a one-and-a-half volt dry battery? Or perhaps they are killing the effects they search for, by the experimental protocols they insist on?) At any rate, the comparison shows us that parapsychology needs field studies as well as laboratory work, and the difference in scale between the effects reported in the two different kinds of investigation makes it hard for many people to believe that the field studies have been correctly reported.

The second reason why scientists who accept the findings of parapsychology are in a minority is more important. It is that we still do not have a theory which will enable the parapsychological facts and the facts of old-fashioned physical science to fit into a single over-arching system. We are still waiting for our Copernicus or our Einstein. Physical science at the beginning of the twenty-first century is a great deal more flexible than it was at the beginning of the twentieth. Chance and probability have taken over from a rigid mechanistic determinism. There are quantum leaps and the findings of chaos theory. But all we have so far in the way of parapsychological theory is a set of suggestive pointers without the detailed mathematical work to show that there are ways in which the psychic data and the physical data are simply sub-sets of a wider understanding of nature and our place within it. Perhaps this new century will bring it. Until we have that theoretical underpinning of this puzzling collection of data, we will not be taken seriously by the majority of scientists. And, even when the right theoretical underpinning has been discovered, we are likely to face just as severe a backlash of conservative thinking as Copernicus or Einstein had to face.

If, in the next few years, some scientific genius can provide an acceptable theory to link normal and paranormal events, then we shall be at the beginning of a very exciting century. It will certainly be as exciting as the century that has just passed. Our descendants may say, in a hundred year's time, what we say about

A parapsychological pilgrimage

the nineteenth century. 'It must have been exciting - if confusing', we say, 'to have lived when the discoveries of Darwin were shaking the foundations of science and religion'. In a century's time, they will be saying, 'It must have been exciting to live at the beginning of the twenty-first century, when the discoveries of parapsychology began to be integrated into our understanding of how the universe works'.

#

How does one begin to learn about all these exciting avenues of thought? How did it work out for *me*? My own parapsychological pilgrimage took me, first to the scientific basis for asserting that there was anything at all to investigate, then to its ramifications for religious thought and Christian living.

Almost immediately after reading Tyrrell and delivering my talk to the school Scientific Society, I joined the Society for Psychical Research as a Student Associate and began to read as widely as I could in the back numbers of its publications. The SPR had been founded in the heyday of late-Victorian scientific optimism by a group of Cambridge scholars in 1882, to

> examine without prejudice and prepossession and in a scientific spirit those faculties of man, real or supposed, which appear to be inexplicable on any generally recognised hypothesis.

It holds no corporate view about the phenomena which it investigates, but acknowledges in its publications nowadays the claim that

> it has for over a century published an impressive body of evidence for the existence of such faculties and the occurrence of paranormal phenomena.

As a fledgling scientist, I was attracted by its stance of investigating anything, but accepting nothing until it was conclusively proved. I found the mixture of open investigation and discriminating examination much to my liking, and have remained a member ever since. The subject needs a strongly critical stance. There is so much in it which is counter-intuitive to the scientifically-trained mind; and yet, without an open mind which is prepared to examine the evidence, how can we ever learn anything new? One's mind needs to be open, but it is essential not to let one's brains fall out of the hole. It seemed to me that the SPR had got just about the right mixture of openness and incredulity to be able to make some progress in this new and difficult field of study.

But before long, my interest in the whole field began to widen out. I started off as a young person with a religious faith and a scientific education who wanted to read all about parapsychology because it offered a way of intellectual understanding between the two disciplines. But when I became ordained, and as I wrote about the subject, and spoke about it at various meetings, I began actually to *meet* people who wanted to tell me about their strange (sometimes disturbing, sometimes enlightening) psychic experiences, and who wanted help in coming to terms with them.

I soon began to discover that a high degree of psychic awareness is far from being an unmixed blessing. Some people seem to be so psychically 'open' that they feel the pains of everybody they meet, or are psychically bombarded with more information that they can easily handle. The emotional and spiritual stresses this causes can be very difficult to deal with. People with psychic gifts need a specialised kind of pastoral care. What had begun for me as an intellectual quest was developing in much more of a pastoral direction, though it had perforce to be fitted within the interstices of a very busy life, successively as curate, lecturer, publisher, archdeacon, and bishop's chaplain.

But what a variety of people I came across, and what a variety of experiences!

There was the retired High Court judge who told me how he had seen an apparition of his younger brother at the time of his death several thousand miles away. There was the Jesuit who went on retreat and saw a colleague of his walking on the terrace and reading his breviary, then discovered a few hours later that the colleague had died in a road accident some miles away at the precise moment he (thought he?) saw him. There was the clergyman who sat at his table with a pen in his hand and a sheet of

A parapsychological pilgrimage

paper in front of him and discovered that the pen began writing (seemingly of its own volition) messages from his father who had died forty years previously. There was the father-in-law of a senior clergyman who saw his wife sitting in her favourite chair, a month or more after she had died.

People only tell stories like that if they feel they can trust the hearer not to broadcast the news, or (worse) to scoff unbelievingly at an incredible story. Often they are worried that they might be going mad, or that their experiences are the work of the devil, or that nothing like this has ever happened to anybody else ever before in the whole history of the world. They are enormously relieved to be told that things like this are normal (if rare); that although they sometimes can betoken mental illness, the symptoms of that are far different from the phenomena they are reporting; and that their story will be listened to sympathetically and treated with a courteous consideration, though my explanation of what is going on may not be the same as theirs, since I may very often believe that there is a normal rather than a paranormal explanation for their unusual experiences.

Then there have been experiences in houses - some good, some bad, some indifferent. The occasional appearance of an eighteenth-century figure at one of the windows of the ancient manor house where a cousin of mine lived for many years. A feeling of spiritual oppression in a block of flats which had been built on the site of what used to be the mortuary of a parish workhouse. The smell 'like warm wet coal' in a house built where miners' cottages used to stand, and where the man of the house used to come back from the pit and have his bath in a galvanised tub in front of the roaring coal fire. The vision of a group of mediæval peasants carrying a cloth-wrapped bundle through the sitting room of a house in a New Town which was subsequently shown to lie on the route between an ancient village and a plague pit. Poltergeist disturbances on a hospital ward where a new recruit onto the cleaning staff had disrupted what used to be a happy workforce. Similar disturbances in a factory where relationships between management and workforce were more Victorian than twentieth-century. The same kinds of thing happening in a Rectory where a marriage was in the process of breaking up.

I have been called in to bless a student flat where the previous occupants were suspected of occult practices; or a church where the vestry had been used by the church treasurer for the sexual abuse of choirboys; or to say prayers at another church where the altar had been desecrated with satanic symbols.

But psychic awarenesses are not always disturbing. Happier cases are much more common. Many couples with close emotional ties to each other know how they can occasionally pick up each other's thoughts in ways that go beyond normal intuition or customary expectation. Many people have discovered and wondered at the way in which they have been made especially aware of the divine presence or the presence of an angel at some turning-point of their lives. There are many spiritual experiences with a psychic slant to them - some trivial, some exceedingly significant - which people will only tell to another person when they know they can trust them not to scoff or to explain them away.

What has been the attitude of religious authority to all this area of study? It was not long before I found that the established churches took a rather dim view of the subject. Prominent churchpeople had belonged to the SPR. William Boyd Carpenter, Bishop of Ripon at the turn of the century, was one of its Presidents, and W.R. Matthews, Dean of St Paul's, had given the Myers Memorial Lecture to it in the 1940s. But the general view was that it was too near the heretical beliefs of the Spiritualists for Christians to be happy to be counted as interested in it. (Spiritualism began in the 1840s as a religious interpretation of some of the phenomena. Scientific psychical research followed, a generation later, in order to see whether the alleged phenomena actually existed and, if so, to understand them from within a scientific rather than a religious view of the world. Several of the pioneers of psychical research were also Spiritualists, but the two pursuits were of a quite different nature.)

Then I discovered that a body, originally called the Churches'

A parapsychological pilgrimage

Fellowship for Psychical Study, had been founded in 1953. It was some years after its foundation before I discovered it. When I did, I was at first very suspicious of it, because I thought it had deserted the scientific caution of the SPR and adopted the credulity of Spiritualism. It accepted a good many phenomena, and in particular it seemed to accept the interpretation of a good many phenomena, that my education within the SPR had taught me to regard with considerable suspicion.

Not until I was properly introduced to it in the 1970s (by which time it had re-named itself the Churches' Fellowship for Psychical and Spiritual Studies, a title it still holds) did I realise that I was harbouring severe misconceptions about it, and that it was a Fellowship which existed to promote the study of psychical and religious experience within an orthodox Christian context, and that it required its full members and office-holders either to belong to one of the main-stream churches or themselves to acknowledge a personal faith in Jesus Christ as Lord and Saviour of the World. By 1977, Leslie Price, the editor of its theological quarterly the *Christian Parapsychologist*, had asked me to review for his publication, and not long after that, I took over from him as its Editor.

The Fellowship asked me to be its Chairman in 1986 and its President in 1998; and I have had the privilege of editing the *Christian Parapsychologist* for a quarter of a century, which has given me an unparalleled opportunity of assessing Christian thinking on the paranormal over that time. I have discovered in the Fellowship a body of people who have given deep, sustained, and continuous thought on the relationship of psychic claims to Christian theology, and who have also formed a support group for Christians who believe themselves to have received psychic gifts - abilities about which their own churches and congregations have too often been suspicious and unhelpful.

This book has been written to commemorate fifty years of the CFPSS, a unique Christian organisation performing a unique service for members of the churches. I have been known to say, with my tongue in my cheek, that the Fellowship has close on

15,000 members. That is true, but the great majority of them are now dead. With my Christian beliefs, that makes me say that they are still important members with more privileged access to their Lord and mine, so that their work for the Fellowship can be even more significant than the work of those of us who still remain on this earth. Be *that* as it may, the Fellowship is a body of much greater importance and influence than its present membership of less than a thousand might indicate. It exists, not only to support its members and help them understand their psychic experiences within Christian orthodoxy, but to help that very much larger number of people who have experiences which seem strange to them, which they cannot understand, and which they regard as in some sense 'spiritual'. They may or may not be practising members of Christian churches, they may or may not become members of the Fellowship, but if the Fellowship can help them to comprehend what has been happening to them, can show them how to place it within a Christian understanding of the world, and can enable them to be supported by a Christian congregation, God's work will be being done and the Fellowship will be doing what it was founded for.

#

Has my parapsychological pilgrimage brought my religious convictions from the sphere of faith into that of knowledge?

No. The relation between faith and evidence is a subtle one, and we need to spend a little while looking at it. Evidence needs interpretation, and interpretation needs faith. Too often (as in the 'epicycles' which temporarily shored up the Ptolemaic theory of an earth-centred universe) the faith is faith in a bad theory which has really had its day. Sometimes, faith is faith in a brilliant and elegant new idea which strikes its discoverer with the force of a great revelation. And, as happened at first with Einstein's theory of relativity, sometimes that brilliant idea has not got the experimental verification it needs, and yet it seems so *right* to its discoverer that he has faith in it. He cannot doubt that when the experiment is done the result will bear him out.

In other words, faith has its place in all aspects of life. Neither science, nor parapsychology, nor religion is exempt. What we need to do is to observe at what point it enters the argument. This is not so that we can blackball speculation, but so that we can say, 'At this point we are beginning to deal with an hypothesis which is held on faith. It may turn out to be a useful working hypothesis, but it may not; and if our faith in it proves to be misplaced, we had better start looking for a better one'.

The difficulty is that each of us has his or her own selection of things which he or she thinks it not unreasonable to believe in; and our lists are all very individual, idiosyncratic and subjective. The late Renée Haynes invented an engaging term to describe this; it was the 'boggle threshold'. The person who approaches the data has ready-made assumptions as to what he or she can and cannot believe. Up to a certain stage, people can accept the evidence of their own eyes. But then, the mind begins to boggle. Before they reach their boggle threshold, the *prima facie* explanation of the data satisfies them. Thereafter, they can become as devious as they like in finding reasons which seem good to them for insisting that things are not what they seem to be.

Thus, some people have a boggle threshold at a point which allows them to accept the possibility of telepathy. But how much further are they prepared to go? Apparitions which are private to the observer? Apparitions which are shared by the bystander? Precognition? Psycho-kinesis? Poltergeists? Mental mediumship? Physical mediumship? Floating trumpets? Materialisations? Unidentified flying objects which abduct their victims and perform experiments on them before returning them back to the 'normal' world?

All right; they have to stop somewhere. But where, and on what criteria? And do the criteria bear any relation to the cogency of the data or the strength of the evidence? The boggle threshold seems to be an entirely subjective matter. Many people will accept any mental phenomena, but boggle as soon as the physical world is involved. Others will accept anything referring to this world, but as soon as survival after death and communication from beyond it is mentioned, they wriggle like worms on the hook.

There is no end to the possibilities of speculation in seeking a theory to bring sense to the many disparate types of paranormal data. How can we make a rational choice between them?

The scientist's job is not over when he has produced his theory, any more than Archimedes had nothing to do after shouting 'Eureka!' than to retrieve his bath towel. The next job is to devise tests to choose between alternative theories; preferably tests based on predictions which will be different on different theories. We do not seem to have got very far with that in parapsychology yet, because the guaranteed repeatable experiment still eludes us, and without repeatable experiments we cannot make rational choices between theories. All we can do is to amass data and try and find a way of looking at them which makes tolerable sense to us, that is, a way which does not go beyond our personal boggle threshold.

And if the evidence takes us beyond that threshold, and we have no coherent theory to make sense of it? If we are honest, we will then have to say that we suspend our judgement. We have an overall world-view which it has taken us all our lifetime so far to build up and test against the available evidence, and it holds together in a way we find convincing. We are simply not prepared to abandon it on the basis of a few odd observations which do not fit in. If we were to accept them at their face value, it might relieve the pressure at that point, but only at the cost of creating bigger and more intractable pressures elsewhere. So the odd and knobbly bits of evidence are filed, so to say, in the 'pending' tray. We cannot see where they go. We cannot say that they do not exist, but we cannot say they are so crucially important that because of them we have to abandon all the sense we have so far made of the universe.

That is an uncomfortable predicament to be in, but anyone except the most obtusely self-satisfied person has been in it at some point or other. There is not one of us who has a philosophy of life, or a viewpoint on the world of phenomena, which perfectly explains every facet of the observed universe. All of us see through a glass, darkly, and it is disingenuous to deny it.

If, however, the pressure mounts, and the evidence grows, we may find we have to do something about it. Many people have started from a position of pure materialism, but they have then become troubled by things that would not fit into that kind of a world. Eventually, their mental 'pending' tray became uncomfortably crowded, and the attempt to ignore the oddball facts or to fit them into the old picture became less and less convincing. The epicycles became more and more convoluted and incredible, and in the end, there had to be a Copernican revolution.

That is how it happens in science, when a new idea takes over. That is how it happens in parapsychology, when a sceptic is finally convinced. That is how it can happen in religion, where the phenomenon is known as 'conversion', and people have to let a new apprehension of reality engulf them as they find release from the intolerable tensions of maintaining a world-picture without God in it. It is possible to come to a conviction about the nature of humankind, its destiny, and its purpose in the mind of God, through the convergent testimony of many lines of evidence. Some will be human, some scientific, some mystical, and even some parapsychological.

The new viewpoint will not be perfect. There are still difficulties in a parapsychological view of reality, or a theistic view, or a Christian view. For example, I still bow before the mystery of reconciling my view of an omnipotent God of love with the facts of animal suffering, or undeserved and unredemptive human suffering, or the suffering of little children. But the difficulties are less than the difficulty of ditching the whole scheme, because no other scheme will cover half the ground half as well.

So I am a Christian parapsychologist. My overall world-view is one in which my Christian faith and the discoveries of psychic studies come together in a convergent way. Faith, reason, and evidence have produced their subtle amalgam. Whether it is because I was born with a predisposition to think in a particular way, or whether it is the result of having undergone a rigorous scientific training, I am not sure; but what I know about myself is that I am happier with the rational than with the intuitive side of human nature. Oddly enough, that has made me more willing to listen to people whose intuitive side is much more fully developed than mine, and to respect what they tell me about their experiences. But it does make me more inclined to accept a 'normal' than a paranormal explanation for many phenomena, and that will be obvious to anyone who reads onwards from here.

That does not mean that I have no more discoveries to make, and no more adjustments in my thinking to look forward to. If I thought there were no points at which the mounting evidence might ever lead me to reconsider my present views, I would be highly alarmed. I have no wish to become intellectually ossified into a position from which there is no chance of movement and none of growth. I am a man of faith, and I hope that my faith is a reasonable faith which has considered the evidence and has matured in the process; but I take great comfort in some words St Paul once wrote to his friends in Philippi. They were written, not when he was a novice or a recent convert, but as a mature Christian thinker towards the end of his life. It was not, he said, as if he had already attained or were already perfect. 'This one thing I do', he wrote; 'forgetting those things that are behind, and reaching forth unto those things that are before, I press toward the mark for the prize of the high calling of God in Christ Jesus' (Philippians 3:12ff). Hold to Christ; but always be on the move!

#

It should by now be obvious that I believe that the scientific study of parapsychology ought to have its effect on Christian theology, and that contacts with people who have had psychic experiences of one sort or another ought to have a bearing on the pastoral work of Christian ministers and on the spirituality of Christian believers. In the rest of this book I want, therefore, to look at some places where the data of parapsychology, an understanding of the Christian faith, and the practice of Christian living can illuminate each other. Although the spiritual is incomplete without the psychical, the psychical is worse than useless without the spiritual. For a full understanding of our life within this exciting world of God's creation, we need both.

2

'What a piece of work is a man!'

What are the components of a human being? We sometimes talk about 'keeping body and soul together'. Each year in London there is a great 'Festival of Body, Mind and Spirit'. We contrast 'flesh and blood' with the more 'spiritual' side of human nature. Into how many parts can we divide ourselves?

It is a question which has been with us for a very long time. Twenty-four centuries ago, as the philosopher Socrates was about to drink the hemlock which was to poison him, he said that 'When death attacks a man, the mortal portion of him may be supposed to die, but the immortal retires at the approach of death and is preserved safe and incorruptible'. His friend Crito asked him how he would like to be buried. 'In any way you like', he replied; 'but you will have to catch me first, and take care that I do not run away. You are burying my body only'.

The idea of the separability of something called the 'soul' from what we know as our physical body is an idea which stems from the ancient Greek philosophers. Whoever it was who wrote the *Wisdom of Solomon* in the Apocrypha of our Bibles was thinking in a very Greek way when he said (9.15) that 'a perishable body weighs down the soul, and its frame of clay burdens the mind already so full of care'. Indeed, he believed that he had a soul which had existed long before it entered into his earthly body. 'As a child,' he wrote (8. 19-20), 'I was born to excellence, and a noble soul fell to my lot; or rather, I myself was noble, and I entered into an undefiled body'. In other words, what constituted the 'I', the person, was not his fleshly body but his immaterial soul.

Psychical and Spiritual

Many of our human experiences bear out this belief in our dual nature. For instance, some people have had what is known as an 'out-of-the-body experience'. Occasionally, the experience came to them as schoolchildren. They were so uninterested in what was going on at the front of the class that they became bored out of their minds and found themselves looking down from the classroom ceiling onto their physical bodies below. And they identified them-'selves' with the observing 'body', not with the inert piece of flesh and bones below.

More usually, out-of-the-body experiences happen when the physical body is undergoing a massive and painful trauma. It is as if the mind can take no more pain, and the overload results in the consciousness of the person disengaging itself from the torments which the body is suffering, and floating freely up to a vantage-point from which it can observe, with a sense of completely disinterested detachment, what is happening down below.

In recent years, we have heard a great deal about the near-death experience, of which an out-of-the-body phase is one part. People who have been resuscitated after cardiac arrest tell of what has been happening to them whilst they have been apparently unconscious, and the stories are quite amazing. Not that this is at all new. Plato wrote about the near-death experience of a soldier named Er who was left for dead on a battlefield, and Bede in the seventh century AD wrote about a man called Drychthelm who had all sorts of adventures whilst in a deathly faint. It is simply that modern medical techniques have made resuscitation possible in many situations where a generation ago death would have been inevitable, so that stories like this, which once would have been rare in the extreme, are now almost commonplace.

It all reinforces the belief that 'body' and 'soul' are separate and separable, and that they are only linked during this earthly life, which is but one episode within a greater immortality.

If so, then perhaps it might be possible to observe, or even to measure, the soul as it separates at the moment of death? Many people claim to have seen something rising from a body and leaving it with a person's dying breath. Victorian lithographs of death-bed scenes depict it dramatically. The same thing happens to some people even today. The newsletter for March 1995 of the Alister Hardy Society, part of the Religious Experience Research Centre, contained a report by Mary Cook of what she saw at her mother's funeral. 'Feeling her soul was still with the body', she wrote,

> I prayed in my spirit that my mother's soul be released in the church with love, gently, and not by force at the crematorium. Then, sideways out of the coffin came, the size of the body, but not the shape, an essence in rays of silver light. This essence stayed whole and drifted up towards the apex of the church, above the altar, and disappeared.

It was not until the very beginning of the twentieth century, however, that scientists tried the bizarre experiment of weighing a patient as he lay dying, in order to see how much weight he lost at the moment of death. In 1901, a certain Dr Duncan MacDougall of Boston, Massachusetts reckoned that, in this way, he had shown that the soul weighed between ten and forty grams.

The difficulty with that kind of experiment is that, as Mary Cook's account reminded us, we do not know whether the soul leaves at the moment of death, or at the funeral, or even later. Death is more of a process than an event which can be timed to the second. That did not stop other doctors repeating MacDougall's experiment, but there was very little consistency in their results. One German experiment found the soul's weight to be no more than ten milligrams. All this might suggest that the doctors concerned were barking up the wrong tree in trying out the experiment at all. If the soul is the immaterial part of a human being, we would not expect it to have any material weight.

#

If the soul has no weight, though, how can it exist at all? What sort of an entity is it? And are we right in thinking of ourselves as a mixture or amalgam of various parts, such as 'soul' and 'body'?

Psychical and Spiritual

We are thrown right in at the deep end of an age-old philosophical problem. René Descartes in the seventeenth century thought the soul resided in the pineal gland at the base of the brain. The Victorians joked 'What is mind? No matter. What is matter? Never mind'. A.J. Ayer and Gilbert Ryle in the mid-twentieth century told us there was no 'ghost in the machine' and that the whole problem was due to a semantic confusion. But whatever they say, we are still faced with the fact that we know intuitively that our body is one kind of thing and our consciousness is another; and it seems that neither can be satisfactorily described or explained in terms of the other.

Let us leave the problem there for the moment, though we will need to come back to it before we get to the end of this chapter. We have noted that we get into difficulties if we try to think of a human being as a compound or amalgam of a number of separate and separable parts such as body, mind, soul, spirit, or whatever words we use for them. Perhaps another tack altogether might prove more profitable? Instead of treating words like 'soul' and 'spirit' as descriptive of parts of the total human being, let us ask what we are *doing* when we use words like this.

It will be helpful if we begin a bit further back. There are various words which sound at first as though they are describing substances, but are in fact describing relationships. You might think that anything you can 'make' is a substance or an object. So, when I cook meat and vegetables together, I 'make' a stew. When I place paper and wood and coal in the grate and put a match to it, I am making a fire. But when I make haste, what am I manufacturing? Or when I make merry? Or when I make love? We can make love, but love is not a substance or an object. It is an attitude shown in relationships. Love is what happens between people who are in a relation to each other.

'Grace' is another word which is often assigned to the wrong category. We think of it as some *thing* which God gives out to us (as in that reputed Scots prayer, 'Lord, give us grace, or we will not give thee glory; and who would be the better for that, Lord?'). But grace is not a *thing* of which we can have more or less. Despite the greeting, 'Hail, Mary, full of grace', grace is not a substance of which the Blessed Virgin could be filled. God's grace is a description of God's attitude towards us, or a description of the relationship he wishes to have with us. God acts towards us in a gracious way; God wishes to have a gracious relationship with us. That is what God's grace is about.

'Love' and 'grace' are words which looked at first as if they were things or substances, but which we see are really about relationships or values. Could the same be true of words like 'body' and 'soul' and 'flesh' and 'spirit'?

That certainly seems to be the case when we look at the way in which St Paul used these terms in his correspondence. He does not use them to designate specific and separable parts of the total human being. He uses them to describe different aspects of the whole person in relation to God.

When we use the word 'body', we usually mean the physical part of a human being as distinct from any mental or spiritual part. We talk, for example, about 'keeping body and soul together'. But when St Paul used the Greek word σωμα (*soma*), which we usually translate as body, he did not have that kind of background idea at all. For him, *soma* was a word which denoted the whole person; not something we *have*, but what we *are*.

What is true of the Greek of St Paul is also true of the Hebrew of the Old Testament. The word *nephesh* occurs about five hundred times in the Old Testament. In the King James version, it is translated four hundred times as 'soul' and a hundred times as, simply, 'life'. In fact, there was, in Old Testament times, no word for 'body' in contrast to 'soul'. What there were, were different words describing the whole human person in different ways - some terms emphasising their vitality and others their mortality. Using the word *nephesh* meant that the writer was referring to a human being - a whole and indivisible human being - as alive.

Paul was a Hebrew deeply influenced by Greek ideas and Greek culture, but he retained his Hebraic background rather than any Socratic philosophy when he used the word *soma*. It is the nearest equivalent we have to our word 'personality'. That word, in the sense of 'the assemblage of qualities or characteristics which makes a person a distinctive individual', does not appear in the older Bible translations. According to the *New Shorter Oxford English Dictionary*, it was not so used before the late eighteenth century.

Because the men who produced the King James Version did not have the word 'personality' to use, but had to translate *soma* as 'body', that phrase 'the resurrection of the body' can be so misleading. Mediæval theologians got into a real lather over what happened to the material particles of our bodies when they rose again at the Last Day. Did they regain all those little bits that had been lost during their owners' earthly lifetimes? It was a matter of debate whether the resurrected body of Jesus of Nazareth, who was a circumcised Jew, did or did not contain the little bit that was snipped off it when he was eight days old. Had the mediævals possessed the term 'personality', and had they spoken of 'the resurrection of the personality', they would have been closer to the meaning of St Paul and could have saved themselves a great deal of trouble.

The same kind of thing happens when we look closely at the word 'flesh'. When we use it, we think, for instance, of a human body made of flesh and blood. We remember what a pickle Shylock got himself into when he asked for a pound of flesh without specifying the blood that went with it. St Paul did not use the Greek word σαρξ (*sarx*), which we translate 'flesh', like that. *Sarx*, for Paul, is the word he uses when he wants to emphasise that a human being can live a life at a distance from God. When a person is concerned with external and visible things, rather than with those which are internal and spiritual, that person is living 'according to the flesh'. 'For I know', wrote Paul (Romans 7.18, KJV) 'that in me (that is, in my flesh,) dwelleth no good thing'. He did not mean that there was something wrong with the material of which his physical body was made. He meant that, apart from God, human nature cannot act in a way which gives God any satisfaction.

Because of the way Paul uses it, the word *sarx* has caused great difficulties to twentieth-century Bible translators. 'Lower nature', 'unspiritual self', 'mere human nature', sinful nature', and many other attempts have been made. Professor James Dunn (*The Theology of Paul the Apostle* [1998], page 67) sums the matter up by saying that :

> Paul walks quite a fine line between regarding flesh as irredeemably flawed and treating it as actively antithetic and hostile to God. ... [T]he connecting thread throughout is the weakness and corruptibility of the flesh, so that a life lived on that level or characterized by that level is headed inescapably for death.

Similarly for the word πνευμα (*pneuma*), which we usually translate as 'spirit'. This, again is not *part* of a human being, or something that we could think of as being bolted on at some stage in a person's spiritual development, for example at baptism or as the result of some particular kind of religious experience. *Pneuma*, when it is used of a human being, is something to do with the whole of the person. To quote Professor Dunn again (p.77), the spirit is 'that dimension of the human person by means of which the person relates most directly to God'.

The Hebrew or Greek words which we translate 'spirit' can also mean 'wind' or 'breath', and they speak to us of the creative power of God himself. That verse in the opening chapter of Genesis (1.2), describing the universe on the first day of its creation, contains its calculated ambiguities. Does it say that the earth was then without form and void and the Spirit of God moved on the face of the waters? Or that the earth was a vast waste until an almighty wind swept over it? Or that it had no form until the creative breath of God acted upon it? The ambiguity is deliberate, just as it is in St John's Gospel, where Nicodemus is told (3.8) that the wind blows where it wills, just as it is with those who are born from the Spirit. The word 'spirit' takes us to the creative work of God, and when it is used of a human being, it reminds us of what the Quakers were to call 'that which is of God in every man'.

And ψυχη (*psyche*)? That ought particularly to interest readers of a book entitled *Psychical and Spiritual*. Paul does not use the word very often. When he does, he does not use it in Socrates' sense of something which separates from the body at death, and is inherently immortal. He uses it to mean the whole human being, made by God, of value to God, and loved by God. So, when we translate the word *psyche* as 'soul', we are not talking about a particular element in a compound which we call a human being. We are talking about a whole human being in the sight of God. I do not *have* a soul, as I have a heart or a liver or a pineal gland; I am a soul. The word 'soul' is a shorthand term for the value in God's sight of this human pattern of matter and energy, genes and experiences, which makes me what and who I am. We can no more weigh the soul, or see it, than we can weigh or see love or loyalty or bravery. Their results can be seen and appreciated; but they themselves are ways of describing the kind of human being a particular human being is. So we should not expect to see the soul leaving the body at the time of death. Or try to weigh it.

What, then, did Mary Cook see at her mother's funeral? What was the nature of that 'essence in rays of silver light' that she saw coming out of the coffin? Perhaps she was a particularly visually-gifted person, and needed to have some visible assurance that her mother was indeed well and would not be harmed by what was to happen in the crematorium. The human 'aura', or visible packet of coloured light which some clairvoyant sensitives claim to see around the bodies of people whom they meet, may be the same. It could be the way in which someone who is a particularly vivid visualiser gives imaginative substance to the telepathic message she receives from a person whose 'aura' she 'sees'.

Similarly, I believe there is no quasi-physical soul which departs from the body at death; but a person who is primarily a visualiser imagines the soul by clothing it in terms of visual imagery. What is 'seen' is seen with the inner eye and would not appear on a photograph; but it gives reality to the conviction that the person whose earthly body is now lifeless, is still alive, because that person is a soul, and is kept in being by a loving God.

If *psyche* in Paul refers to the whole person, as created by God, it means that the abilities to which we are referring when we use the term, 'the psychic faculty', are part of the way in which God has created human beings. And if Paul used words like *psyche* and *pneuma* with different connotations, it warns us that the psychical and the spiritual are not the same, and we do well to differentiate between them. What is psychical is part of God's creation, and, like so many other things in creation, it can either be used or misused. If it is used to God's glory and the good of humanity, it is also spiritual. If it is used for selfish ends, or to make people wonder at the powers and abilities of the person who possesses it, or even (which God forbid) to harm others, it is being misused, and is, in Paul's terms, fleshly rather than spiritual. It is easy for people to be mesmerised by the psychic faculty, and, for instance, to believe that because a statement has been psychically transmitted it must therefore be true and good. But since what is psychic is natural, it is prone to all the sinful impulses to which nature is subject, and what comes through it must be discriminatingly assessed, and never simply accepted without question.

And, since what is psychic is natural, it is not 'occult'. Members of the Churches' Fellowship for Psychical and Spiritual Studies are well used to the sort of ignorant criticism that they are 'dabbling in the occult'. Their critics are wrong on two counts. A body which involves itself in serious and scientific study certainly is not 'dabbling' in anything; and what it studies is not the 'occult'. That word means 'hidden', and refers to a belief that by the possession of secret knowledge, initiates can gain insights into the nature of the universe and its denizens which are not open to the ignorant masses. People who are 'into' the occult may well claim to use psychic powers to further their studies and extend their practices, but to confuse a natural faculty like the psychic with beliefs like those of occultism, is a crass error. Christians, whose doctrines are open for all the world to see, can have no truck with occultism, but they should certainly be able to investigate God-given human natural abilities, such as psychic sensitivity, without risk of censure.

#

All this talk of the way in which terms like body, soul, flesh, and spirit denote values, or relationships between ourselves and God, may sound inescapably theological and pre-scientific; but in fact it resonates remarkably well with modern science by speaking, not of the divisibility, but of the unity, of the whole human being.

And what a remarkable creature, with what remarkable powers, is the human being! As Hamlet exclaimed,

> What a piece of work is a man! How noble in reason! How infinite in faculty! In, form, in moving, how express and admirable! In action how like an angel! In apprehension how like a god! The beauty of the world! The paragon of animals!

And yet, despite this greatness, we can be torn in mutually opposite directions. We can act as though God does not exist and as though he has no call upon us, and if so, we shall be acting 'according to the flesh'. Or we can become aware of our calling as children of God and react to our higher aspirations, in which case the use of the word 'spirit' would be more appropriate. But all the time we are whole human beings, souls, wonderfully made and with a range of quite amazing faculties.

Even the purely animal or mechanical abilities of the human body ought to lead us to a sense of wonder. Somehow, without our conscious intervention, our heart keeps beating, our food is digested, our blood pressure is maintained, oxygen is supplied wherever it is needed, and our bodies keep themselves at a regular 37°C. Of most of this we are entirely unaware unless we stop to think. Most of it we are entirely unable to influence, although, for instance with breathing, there are parts of it over which we can have a limited and temporary degree of control.

We are aware of a world external to ourselves, which we can explore through sight and sound, touch and smell, taste and texture. Our sense receptors are sensitive over an amazing range. For example, the human retina can be stimulated by a single quantum of light, yet it only begins to become overloaded and break down when it is bombarded by more than ten thousand million quanta at a time. But in other respects it is remarkably limited. The range of wave-lengths that the human eye can detect is tiny indeed. We react to light only within a very narrow spectrum. Infra-red, ultra-violet, x-rays, radar waves, or radio waves, all pass by us undetected. The world as perceived by a frog or a bee is vastly different from 'our' world, let alone from the world as perceived by some fish which can detect gradients in electro-magnetic potential. My perceived reality is only a partial perception, chosen out of total reality by the abilities of the human brain and body.

(Indeed, it may be that some paranormal manifestations are correlated with variations in the earth's electro-magnetic field or with the presence of standing waves of an extremely low frequency. That *may* indicate that what we call 'extra-sensory perception' might not be extra-sensory at all, but be quite literally a 'sixth sense' quite different from any of our five 'normal' senses - perhaps a kind of human sensory perception akin to that of those fish which use an electro-magnetic sensor.)

What is even more mysterious than the way in which we are aware of the outside world or of selected aspects of it, is the way in which we are aware of ourselves as selves, and we have an interior world which is private to each one of us. Not only that; we are also able to recognise that the outside world contains other human beings like ourselves, whom we assume to have inner worlds similar to our own, so that we have evolved methods by which we may communicate with them.

And, more mysteriously still, we have feelings and emotions. Some of them are basic and apparently simple, such as contentment, fear, or surprise. Others are more sophisticated, like curiosity. Others we find so deep that it is hard to find words to express them - love, hate, mystery, wonder, the appreciation of great art or music; religious awe. And there is the mystery of rapport between friends or lovers, or (for good or ill) between an orator and his audience.

We have abilities, too. Many of them, such as sight, taste, and sound are innate and automatic. But even these can be developed if we have the desire and the aptitude and are prepared to undergo the training. We all see, but few of us notice. We all hear, but few of us become music critics. We all taste, but not many of us become the kind of expert who can take a glass of wine, and assess its quality and its qualities. We can all kick a ball, but there are very few footballers of international talent. We can all move our fingers, but how many of us could become concert pianists? Most of us can add and subtract, but how few of us are financial wizards?

The same is true in the religious life. If we are to believe the statistics collected by the Alister Hardy Religious Experience Research Centre, over half of the population of England has at some time or other had what they describe as a religious experience; but very few of them have developed that sense of religious awareness which came to them in their moment of insight. Very few have become great mystics, or have explored far into the mysteries of prayer. To aptitude and ability there needs to be added training if anything much is to be made of it.

But even without training, the range of our purely natural abilities ought to amaze us. If, as this book does, we concentrate on those which are commonly designated as 'psychic', we shall be dealing with a vast spectrum of human possibilities. Some of them are universally acknowledged; but the recognition of many of them goes well beyond many people's boggle threshold. We need, as ever, a discriminating and critical approach if we are to distinguish between reality and fantasy.

We communicate by using words; but there are many ways of communication which use no words at all. We can read volumes into a flicker of the eyelid or the most fleeting expression on the face. Often, we are not even aware that we are using a non-verbal method of communication. Some people are more sensitive to such nuances of body language than others, and sometimes they can have so close a rapport with a friend or spouse that it almost seems as if they can read their mind, or know what they are thinking without any need for it to be spoken out loud.

Is that an example of extra-sensory perception, or of extra-sensitive sensory awareness? Most of the time, we shall never know; but researchers in parapsychology have to be especially on their guard against letting tiny and all-but-invisible sensory clues help their subjects score positively in tests. Stage magicians and those who pretend to telepathic powers for purposes of entertainment know just how unobservant most people are, and how the tiniest of cues can be effective.

And yet, there have been long and careful experiments, carried out under the most stringent of protocols, in which all possibility of fraud or of sensory cues has been eliminated, which demonstrate, to all but those with the lowest imaginable boggle threshold, that it is possible for thoughts to pass from one human being to another without the use of any of our normal senses. Telepathy is a fact.

Experimentally speaking, the extent to which telepathy operates seems to be a very low one indeed, so that only sophisticated statistical analysis can show that it has taken place in any particular experiment. It does not seem able to be laid on to order, and it seems to depend very largely on something subtly to do with the 'personal equation' between the experimenter and the subject, and with their mental and emotional state at the time the experiments take place. In other words, telepathy is rare, and there are many more occasions on which it does not take place than there are occasions when it can be shown to have been active. This may indicate that when friends, or a married couple, believe that they have been telepathically aware of what the other has been thinking, it is more likely to be the case that they have developed so close a rapport with each other that they can read each others' non-verbal signals with what seems like uncanny accuracy, or that they know each other so well that they can guess where their thoughts have got to with more than a coincidental chance of being right.

This is not to say that telepathy does not occur; only to say that it may be more rare than many people think. And, just as some people are better at mathematics than others, so some people may be more psychically sensitive than others. This will show in a greater degree of empathy with people they meet, or a more developed sense of intuition. It will also mean they receive telepathic impressions more often than other people. They may be what are known as 'natural psychics'. They cannot help it. They cannot not be aware of the impressions they receive. But the fact that they receive accurate telepathic impressions more often than the average person does not confer infallibility on them. They need to be more careful than other people to test these impressions, and not to rely on them until they are satisfied that they are reliable. A great deal of harm can come from taking the impressions of a natural psychic as though they were always and inevitably gospel truth.

The same is true of premonitions. All of us are aware that accidents can happen, and we know that we may be involved with one, be it at home, on the roads, or on the railway, before the day is out. Most of us have learnt not to make this a cause for worry. But every now and again, there comes a strange kind of warning premonition. 'Don't go to work that way this morning; something horrible will happen to you if you do'. So we change our normal route, and no harm befalls us.

How do we evaluate that sort of thing? How do we know that if we hadn't heeded the warning, we would have come to grief? How do we know that it wasn't just one more irrational worry presenting itself to us in the guise of a premonition, and having no other cause than our fearful nature?

Usually, that is just what it is. But not always. There is an odd statistic which shows that trains which meet with accidents carry fewer passengers than the same trains on adjacent days or on the same day in adjacent weeks. It is as though some small number of people decided, for no apparent reason, not to travel on their usual train on the day of the accident, or to make their journey in some other way.

And there are the disasters which seem to have been foreseen by complete strangers. For instance, the tip at Aberfan which engulfed a school and killed so many innocent children seems to have been precognised by a number of people. Again, some individuals seem to be more prone to receiving such 'warning' dreams or visions than the rest of us are, and it can cause them intense distress because they 'know' that something is about to happen, and they cannot prevent it. Usually they do not know enough about it to do anything useful; the precognition is not precise and definite enough to enable them to take avoiding action, or to warn other people who would be involved were it to be fulfilled. As a lady said to a friend of mine,

> pictures come into my mind - rather like a small television screen just in front of my forehead. At first, I thought it was imagination. But [after one of the visions 'came true'] I realised I'd had some sort of preview. Things like this happen to me every so often, and I'm rather scared, because it's usually a disaster, and I feel somehow responsible.

The whole business of precognition is a puzzle. Time's arrow only goes one way, and it is impossible for an event to come before its cause. Perhaps what is precognised is only one of a number of possibilities. Perhaps what is precognised is an already-existing but unrecognised danger, like the tip at Aberfan which was dangerously unstable for a long time before it collapsed. An analysis of precognitions, reported in the *Journal* of the Society for Psychical Research for October 1995, showed that what is foreseen only comes to pass when the person who has had the precognition either cannot, or does not, do anything to influence the precognised event, or to cause anyone else to influence it. We do not live in a predetermined universe; our freely willed actions can affect the future. A precognition is a warning to do something about a possibility which we do not want to become an actuality.

#

Premonitions are examples of psychic awareness of what might be about to happen in the physical world. There are several other kinds of reported or alleged psychic awareness which have to do with physical matter or material events. It seems, for instance, that some people can indulge in 'remote viewing' in which they are clairvoyantly aware of the details of a distant location. It has been alleged that the US intelligence service carried out experiments during the Cold War period, and discovered that some sensitives could give them accurate information about the disposition of secret Soviet installations. Other sensitives seem able to perform what is known as 'psychometry' - they use phys-

Psychical and Spiritual

ical objects to log on to the former owners of those objects and to find out information about them.

Some people seem to be psychically aware of facts about the places they visit. Many of us feel that certain places, those in which prayer has been offered for century after century, are holy in an almost palpable way. The converse is true, and places which have been used for wrongful purposes, or where intensely unhappy things have happened, can also cast their pall over occupants or visitors who are sufficiently psychically sensitive. Place memories seem to stick to some localities, and can be triggered from time to time, so that they get the reputation of being 'haunted'. Such memories seem to be quasi-physical and to have no remaining personality attached to them, so they can do no harm to those who become aware of them. But if they are the memories of past evil or past distress, it may be necessary to cleanse the spot of its lingering evil, or to ask God (by prayer or requiem Eucharist) to grant peace to those people whose past unhappinesses have stuck to that spot.

What, then, of dowsing? Is that a psychic or a physical reaction? Some people can walk over a piece of ground with a bent twig, and they can tell from the way in which it twitches whether there is underground water, or the remains of ancient buildings. Are they made aware by psychic means, or is it as physical, but as mysterious, as the powers of homing pigeons? The question is even more acute when dowsers, instead of physically walking over an area, work with their rod or pendulum on a map of the district to reveal its hidden features.

Akin to this may be the claim by some sensitives to be able to detect changes in the appearance of people according to their emotional or spiritual state. We have already mentioned the 'aura' and hazarded the guess that it may be a visualisation of information acquired either normally through reading a person's character by non-verbal signals, or paranormally by telepathy. The ancient world knew quite a lot about this, and depicted its saints and holy people with haloes about their heads, or sometimes about the whole of their bodies.

What a piece of work is a man!

I remember as a young man being told by someone from Lincolnshire about Edward King, the saintly bishop of that diocese in late Victorian and Edwardian days. 'His face shone', he said; 'there was no other way of describing it.' When the three disciples saw Jesus transfigured on the mountain-top, with his body and his very clothes shining with a whiteness no earthly laundry could emulate, they may have been giving visual form to a realisation that the person whom they were following was no ordinary mortal.

Then there are people who seem to have a strange gift of healing. They may feel their fingers tingle, or they may have no such sensation. They may feel that 'virtue has gone out from them', or there may be no such feeling. But the people upon whom they lay their hands seem to recover much more rapidly from their illnesses than a control group of others whom they have not treated.

Paranormal healing may be part of the strange business of 'mind over matter', or psycho-kinesis (PK). The pioneering experiments of Dr Rhine in America between the wars asked subjects to 'will' the way in which dice would fall. Nowadays, researchers into PK use random number generators. They have begun to discover that the machines produce truly random series of numbers in normal circumstances, but when they are introduced into a situation that is highly emotionally charged, their output is no longer random.

As usual, the laboratory investigates tiny effects whereas 'real life' comes up with something much more exciting. I remember a theological student telling me that as a teenager she was able to make small objects on her dressing-table move by simply looking at them and willing them to do so. A Russian psychic named Nina Kulagina has made similar claims. Séance-rooms, particularly in the Victorian era, were infamous for their levitations and physical effects, though the advent nowadays of more sophisticated methods of detection has drastically reduced the number of reported claims. A group of friends from the Norfolk village of Scole discovered a couple of sensitives who seemed able, amongst other effects, paranormally to produce marks on a photographic film sealed against interference. The results were published by the Society for Psychical Research in 1999, but are hotly disputed by those who cannot believe they can be genuine (the boggle threshold again?).

And what the parapsychologists call RSPK (repetitive spontaneous psycho-kinesis) but the rest of us know as the poltergeist, is still very much with us. It appears that a situation of emotional stress in a household or work situation can cause physical phenomena like loud bumps, changes in temperature, malfunctioning of electronic devices, and the disappearance, replacement, and movement of objects, which are usually small knick-knacks, but sometimes quite large pieces of furniture. Again, the facts are disputed, and some investigators believe that the physical movements are all either imaginary or fraudulent, artefacts of the psychological disturbance which surrounds them. But that the phenomena happen, whatever their explanation, is not in doubt.

#

Human faculties seem to have a wider scope than we could have imagined. And as yet we have made no mention of the way in which it seems possible for some people to communicate with disembodied human beings who have passed through the barrier of death.

In the early days of psychical research, a great deal was made of anecdotal cases of what came to be known as 'crisis apparitions'. Particularly in the days when travel was slow and communications from abroad took days to arrive, there were many stories told of people who saw the figure of their friend or spouse or child at exactly the time of their death (or, less usually, a serious accident) in a distant country, so that when the news came through, it simply confirmed what the person who had seen the apparition already realised. Cases like this are less often reported today, perhaps because news of disasters nowadays comes virtually instantaneously. In any case, the stories are no evidence for the survival after death of the person whose apparition was seen. They can indicate that the person who saw the apparition was telepathically reminded of their loved one at the same time as that loved one was undergoing some great trauma, but unless they passed on some other unknown but verifiable information, that is the most they could be held to prove.

Similarly, when a widow sees her former husband, sometime after his death, sitting in his familiar armchair, it may be no more than a bereavement hallucination. The widow may take it as an indication that he is still in some way alive and that the bond of love between them is unbroken (and she may well be correct in this), but such a conviction is in the nature of faith rather than proof.

What, then, of one of the highest-profile examples of psychic sensitivity, that of mediumship? It looks as if some people can make contact with those who have passed beyond this mortal life and can tell us what they are thinking or experiencing in the post-mortem state. Usually this is done verbally, in a mild trance state, though some practitioners hold a pen or pencil in their hands over a blank sheet of paper, and allow it to write of its own accord. Others use planchette or the ouija board, which allows an upturned glass or some other object to point to words or letters in such a way as to spell out an answer to a question or give a message, allegedly from a departed spirit.

Undoubtedly, the majority of such communications are not what they purport to be. The ouija board (the use of which is not to be recommended - see page 94 below) may work by the familiar psychological method of 'projection'. This is a psychological trick in which a person's repressed subconscious material comes out into the open; but it cannot be consciously recognised as such. Instead, it is disguised as though it came, not from the operator, but from a discarnate being. Similarly, mediumistic statements are often not what they appear to be. A medium may have a dissociated personality, part of which can temporarily split itself off from her conscious mind and spin likely stories which have no more arcane source than her own unacknowledged inner fantasies. Many mediums are expert at 'cold reading'. They can interpret their clients' body language, or make correct inferences from inadvertently-disclosed information. Clients are often so desperate for messages from their departed loved ones that they impart personal significance to bland statements which might be true of half the population.

But there are the exceptional mediums, who seem uncannily to be able (on occasions, and not infallibly) to make verifiable statements about things which were unknown to the sitter but relevant to the person who was ostensibly communicating. It does look as though, sometimes, the veil between this world and the next is drawn aside for a tantalising moment, and information passes across. It happens rarely, but we must allow for the fact that it can happen. And if it happens in the rare, documented, verifiable cases, we should also allow that it may be happening on some of the many less formal occasions when nothing objectively verifiable is coming across, but a likely scenario is being described. It all makes Hamlet's astonished exclamation 'What a piece of work is a man! ... How infinite in faculty!' even more obviously true.

#

If we are considering some of the abilities of the human being, we need also to look in a spiritual direction. Can we be aware, not only of the creation, but of the Creator? Can we carry on a conversation, not only with humans, but with the divine? Can we receive messages, not only from worldly sources, but from a realm beyond this visible one? Is there some objective reality to the mystical states which are reported, or to the numinous religious feelings which so many of us have at peak moments in our lives, or to the sense of inner enlightenment which can result from meditative techniques?

There is, of course, objective reality to them in the sense that they are accompanied by detectable brain states. The last few years have seen an amazing leap forward in our understanding of the human brain, and research is going on so fast that anything written now is sure to be out of date within a very few years. What neurophysiologists are beginning to discover makes some

What a piece of work is a man!

of the most exciting reading in modern science.

We now know that every human brain is an incredibly complex system of billions of neurones, some linked by electrically-conducting fibres and others triggered by microscopic squirts of psychoactive chemicals.

Early on, researchers realised that particular areas of the brain were responsible for particular functions. One part of the brain was used for moving the limbs, for example, and another one for keeping the heart beating. Then the discovery was made that, when particular areas of the brain were stimulated, the patient began to perceive particular sensations such as sounds, smells, sights, memories. Not only that, but the two hemispheres of the brain were found to have different functions. The left one was more mathematical and logical whilst the right was more intuitive and imaginative. Early in the twentieth century, the German theologian Rudolf Otto had tried to describe the sense of the numinous in words, and had had to admit that it could be evoked but not expressed. Now we are beginning to realise that the reason for this is that the numinous is primarily a right-hemisphere function and the words with which we try to encapsulate it are primarily from the other hemisphere, so that they are inadequate for a right-hemisphere task.

But it soon became apparent that emotions are due not to specific parts of the brain but to interactions between more than one part. The sense of mystical enlightenment, for instance, comes about because the act of meditation sets up a kind of reverberating brain circuit, as Eugene d'Aquili and Andrew Newberg explain on pages 111-112 of their book *The Mystical Mind* (Fortress Press, 1999):

> Impulses originating in the right attention association area, go to the right orientation association area, to the right hippocampus, to the right amygdala, to the quiescent parts of the hypothalamus, and then back to the right amygdala ... Impulses go around and around this circuit, recruiting greater neural activity. ... which results in spillover and instantaneous maximal stimulation of the arousal system. ... [This] results in ecstatic and blissful feelings through intense stimulation of the quiescent structures in the hypothalamus.

Is that all? Are our religious feelings, and all our other emotions, reducible to the stimulation of neurones and synapses? To say so is only one stage more sophisticated than claiming that the human body is simply a mix of chemicals, containing enough iron to make a bag of nails, and enough phosphorus to fill a box of matches. If so, then Hamlet was right to reduce man's nobility of reason and god-like apprehension to no more than quintessence of dust.

That would be one way of understanding the totality of human nature. But it is not the only way, and it misses out on the most significant aspects. The great temptation for all scientists is to fall from science into what has been called 'scientism', which is the belief that by the application of scientific method to a problem, we have exhausted its significance and totally explained its meaning. But scientific method is only one way of understanding the world, and it lets a great deal escape it. It is rather like using a net with a three-inch mesh to trawl the ocean, analysing your catch, and announcing that there are no creatures less than three inches long in the sea.

The brain scientists are unlocking the secrets of how our perceptions, our thoughts and our emotions are linked to chemical and electrical changes within our skulls. We are physical beings, and we can know, feel, or experience absolutely nothing without a brain. In our present embodied state we cannot have thoughts; we cannot be conscious of anything; we cannot be conscious of our selves as selves, let alone of anything impinging upon us from the outside world; without brain activity. The excitement of contemporary neurophysiology is the way in which it is discovering the mechanisms by which all this comes to be. But a thought is not the same as a resonating circuit between neurones. The circuit is there, and the thought cannot come to consciousness without it; but the thought and the circuit are entities of totally different orders. Thoughts may be 'all in the mind', but the mind is not 'all in the brain'. Brain states are not the same as conscious experiences. Brain states are 'third-person' descriptions of what is going on, observed by outsiders with electro-encephalographs or whatever. Conscious experiences are 'first-person' descriptions. Understanding how the brain functions tells us nothing about what it is *like* to have an experience.

An analogy might be between the scene in a television studio and what we see on our screens at home. We cannot see what is going on in the studio without the incredibly complicated mechanism within our television set, and if we damage the set we distort (or even destroy) the picture that it shows. What goes on in the studio and what we see at home is closely connected, but they are not the same thing, and although the programme can exist without our set, the set is no use if there is not a programme for it to tune in to. Similarly, the mind cannot express itself in this world without the brain, but mind and brain belong to different kinds of worlds.

Another analogy, developed by Dr Max Velmans in his book *Understanding Consciousness* (Routledge, 2000), is the difference between a programme on the TV and a piece of video-tape. The tape may contain the same information as the programme we watch when we play it; but it is encoded, and in a different medium, and needs the appropriate machine (a VCR) to decode it. Similarly, the brain holds encoded physical information which the mind needs to decode if it is to turn it into mental experience.

Consciousness is even more of a mystery than brain physiology, and the most sophisticated of philosophers have not yet succeeded in cracking it to the satisfaction of anyone except followers of their particular school. Descartes taught us to think of mind and brain as quite different things which interacted in some mysterious fashion in the pineal gland in the centre of the brain. That no longer satisfies most contemporary thinkers. Nowadays, some people believe that mind is primary and matter no more than an illusion spun out of thought, but most people think that it is matter which is primary, and that one day we shall know so much about the workings of the human brain that we shall be able to describe sight, or sound, or smell (or pain, or love, or mystical rapture) totally in terms of neurones, synapses, and psycho-active chemicals. It is common nowadays to suggest that consciousness is an 'emergent' property which manifests automatically as soon as a creature's brain has grown into a sufficiently complicated structure. The quotation I gave above from Drs d'Aquili and Newberg might be interpreted in this way, though its authors disavow so reductionist an interpretation. In any case, to speak of consciousness as 'emergent' leaves us with the puzzle still there. It tells us nothing about how an experiencing mind and a physical brain can be related.

Dr Velmans does not believe that either matter or mind is the one single basic fact by which we can explain the other. He holds that brain and mind are complementary realities, one described from a third-person perspective and the other by the first person, but in essence two different and alternative ways of talking about the same reality, which is greater than either brain on its own or mind on its own. Atomic physicists know that the electron can be described as a wave or a particle according to the kind of experiment to which they subject it. But an electron is an electron, not divisible or separable into either a wave or a particle. So brain and mind are mind-brain, as indivisible and inseparable as space-time or electro-magnetism. It is an interesting speculation, but in the end, is it any more than verbal sleight-of-hand? The mystery remains.

We may still legitimately believe that the brain is more than an instrument for creating consciousness, and that it can also transmit messages from other realms and dimensions, and put us in touch with transcendent realities such as angels, archangels, the hosts of heaven, and even the Creator of all.

Modern quantum physics allows a single area of space to contain more than one set of particles. Worlds can co-exist in an interlocking series of dimensions. It is pure scientism, not legitimate science, to say that the human being is 'nothing but' its brain and the mechanisms which are being discovered within it, or that the brain and the mind are 'simply' different aspects of a unitary 'mind-brain', so that the physical world is closed to all influences from a supposed world outside it, and self-explanatory in its own terms. Such 'nothing-buttery' misses out on the divine reality which lies hidden behind the phenomenal world. There is a neuro-physiological reason for the feelings of numinous awe, or of *satori* (enlightenment) or of ecstasy; but the deeper reason for them is that as human beings, we are *capax dei* - able to connect with God himself, the God who created material bodies in such a way that they could, over countless millennia, evolve until their physical structures became such as to be able consciously to apprehend spiritual realities.

And those strange paranormal powers which some people seem to have, some more than others? Do they bring us any closer to the God who made us and who wishes to have commerce with us? Sometimes. Many members of the Churches' Fellowship for Psychical and Spiritual Studies have been pitchforked, as the result of a paranormal experience, into a realisation that there is more to life than material things, and have used that experience to begin an exploration of the nature of reality which passed from the psychical into the spiritual.

But we need to beware. Many saints and religious figures have found that their devotional practices led to strange paranormal manifestations. Indeed, in the Roman Catholic Church, a person cannot be advanced to sainthood without evidence of more than one miracle associated either with their life or their relics. But the paranormal manifestations can very easily act as distractions from the path of true spiritual growth. Eastern holy men call them *siddhis* and believe that only charlatans treat them as the most important manifestation of growth towards holiness. The Shorter Catechism of the Presbyterian church is right. The 'chief end' of humanity is not to acquire psychic powers but 'to glorify God and enjoy him for ever'.

In that conviction, let us, in the remaining chapters of this book, look at some of the findings of parapsychology and see what relevance they have for Christian faith and the Christian life.

3

The Bible tells me so

If we were to expunge all accounts of the apparently paranormal from the pages of the Bible, we would be left with an intolerably emasculated volume. When Bibles are laid open, there are millions of surprises! In this chapter, we will first look at the sort of accounts of paranormal happenings the Bible contains. That investigation, however, will leave us with a large number of questions to answer. Did the writers intend us to take them literally or not? If they *did* intend them to be taken literally, can present-day educated Western readers believe them? And what is the attitude of the Biblical writers to the paranormal powers that they tell us about?

#

Any exhaustive account would require a large volume to itself. We can do no more here than give a 'sampler'.

Extra-sensory awareness. Samuel the prophet is able to tell Saul that his father's lost donkeys have been found, and he goes on from this to foretell with uncanny accuracy what will happen to Saul on his way back to his father's house (1 Samuel 10). The prophet Elisha knows what his servant Gehazi is doing, even without being told (2 Kings 5.26). On one occasion, the Aramæan king complains that the King of Israel knows more about his battle-plans than he ought to, and asks who is the secret agent in his camp. One of his staff officers replies, 'None of us, my lord king; but Elisha, the prophet who is in Israel, tells the king of Israel the very words you speak in your bedchamber' (2 Kings

6.11f). Philip persuades Nathanael to come and see the man who had been foretold by the ancient prophets, and Jesus of Nazareth tells Nathanael that he saw him under the fig-tree before Philip spoke to him. Nathanael is so amazed at this that he cries out that Jesus must be the Son of God (John 1.48ff.). On several occasions it is said that Jesus knew what other people were thinking (e.g. Matthew 9.4, John 2.24-5). He was able to astonish the woman by the side of the well in Samaria by telling her that he knew she had had five husbands and that she was not married to her present partner (John 4.18).

Precognition. We have already mentioned the strange case of Saul and Samuel. When Saul left the prophet, he was told that he would meet two men by Rachel's tomb who would tell him that his father's donkeys had been found; then, at the terebinth of Tabor, he would see three men going up to worship God at Bethel, of whom one would be carrying three young goats, the second three loaves, and the third a skin of wine. And so it happened. No wonder that when Saul got as far as the hill of God where the Philistine governor resided, and he saw a company of prophets coming down from the shrine, as Samuel had foretold, he felt the divine hand upon him and was himself overcome by prophetic rapture. Jesus of Nazareth seems to have been particularly able accurately to foretell the future. He repeatedly predicts his own death and the manner of it (e.g. Matt. 20.17ff.). He tells Peter that he will catch a fish with a coin in its mouth (Matt. 17.27). He foretells what will happen to Jerusalem when it is sacked by the invading armies (Mark 13, Matthew 24, Luke 21). On the other hand, Paul in Philippi was so annoyed at the activities of a young female fortune-teller, who was making a nuisance of herself by her frequent activity, that he banished the 'spirit of divination' from her (Acts 16.16-19).

Psycho-kinesis. The magicians of Pharaoh entered into a contest with Moses, who used the powers of his brother Aaron to perform some amazing psycho-kinetic feats (Exodus, chapters 7-9). In many cases, the Egyptian magicians were able to duplicate what Aaron did. When Aaron turned his rod into a serpent, they could do the same. But Aaron always managed to trump them; in this instance, by making his serpent swallow theirs. Eventually, they abandoned the unequal contest because when Moses turned soot from a kiln into a fine dust, it produced such festering boils throughout the land that Pharaoh's magicians were no longer a match for their Hebrew rivals. There are plenty of other reports of psycho-kinesis in Old and New Testaments. The Israelites were able to cross the Red Sea on dry land because God made the waters recede (Exodus 14.21), and Elijah was similarly able to part the waters of the Jordan by miraculous means (2 Kings 2.8). Gideon asked the Lord for a series of signs to prove his mission, and the disposition of dew between a fleece and the surrounding ground was, repeatedly, as Gideon had asked it should be (Judges 6.36-40). Elisha's servant lost the head of his axe in a pond and the prophet made the iron swim (2 Kings 6.6). When Jesus died, the veil of the Temple miraculously tore in two from top to bottom (Mark 15.38). A number of nature-miracles seem to involve psycho-kinetic powers. For instance, the sun's shadow is reported to have gone backwards on the stairway of Ahaz (Isaiah 38.8), and the sun was darkened at the Crucifixion around the time of the Paschal full moon, when an eclipse would have been impossible (Mark 15.33). Jesus was able, so the Gospel-writers aver, to walk on water (Matthew 14.25-9). Then there is the miraculous multiplication of food, recorded both of Elisha (2 Kings 4.42-44) and of Jesus. The feeding of the multitude is the only miracle recorded in all four Gospels (Matthew 14, Mark 6 and 8, Luke 9, John 6), and, as St Mark emphasises (Mark 8.19-21), it happened more than once. On another occasion, Jesus is reported to have turned several gallons of water into wine of superlative quality (John 2. 1-10).

Teleportation is when a person is moved from one place to another by paranormal means. Elijah was carried off to heaven in a whirlwind (2 Kings 2.11); Ezekiel was lifted from Jerusalem to be with the exiles in Babylon (Ezekiel 3.14-15); and Philip was 'caught up' in the desert and deposited in Azotus (Acts 8.39-40). Or were some of these occasions out-of-body experiences rather than descriptions of the relocation of the physical body?

The near-death experience (NDE) is not unknown in the Bible. Paul was stoned at Lystra and left for dead (Acts 14.19), and it may have been on this occasion that he had the vision of the third heaven about which he writes in 2 Corinthians 12.1-4 (though he endured so many floggings and beatings in the course of his journeyings that it may have been on another occasion altogether). He tells us that when this happened, he did not know whether he was in the body or out of the body, and we know that the NDE is often accompanied by an out-of-body experience. And he tells us that then, he 'heard words so secret that human lips may not repeat them'. That sounds like an experience involving the right hemisphere of the brain. Words are processed in the left hemisphere, and a right-hemisphere experience can be ineffable in that all attempts to describe it in words fail. People who have had an NDE often say that they cannot describe verbally what happened to them. There may also be references to an NDE in Psalm 23 ('the valley of the shadow of death'), or Ecclesiasticus 51.6 ('I came very near to death, close to the brink of the grave'). This last may, however, simply imply that the writer had been in great danger of death, either through accident, illness, or the activities of his enemies.

Some commentators have even seen Biblical reports of *Unidentified Flying Objects* in the visions of Ezekiel (1.4-28), or the pillar of cloud by day and fire by night which accompanied Moses and the Israelites on their long journey back to the Promised Land, though I doubt whether that reading of the evidence is likely to satisfy many readers.

Auras or paranormal lights around the heads or bodies of people are reported in Exodus 34.29 where the skin of Moses' face shone after he came down from the mountain, or in Acts 6.15, where the face of Stephen shone like that of an angel. The Transfiguration (Matthew 17) is another example of the same kind of phenomenon, when Jesus' face shone and his clothes became dazzling white; and, of course, the vision reported by St Luke (24.4) at the tomb where the body of Jesus had lain was of two men (or angels?) in dazzling clothes.

Divination has been known from the earliest times. Joseph had a cup which he used for this purpose (Genesis 44. 5,15). The sacred lot was frequently used to determine the will of Jahweh; sometimes in order to discover who was responsible for what had been happening amiss, sometimes to determine who ought to be chosen for a particular task or office. There are several examples of this in the time of King Saul. After all, Saul had himself been chosen to be king over Israel because Samuel had interpreted the sacred lot, first to indicate the tribe of Benjamin, then the family of Matri, then Saul of the sons of Kish (1 Samuel 10.20-24). So when, on a later occasion, Saul enquired of the Lord as to whether he should pursue the fleeing Philistines, and the sacred methods of divination gave him no answer, he believed it was because someone had not obeyed his instructions to avoid eating until after the battle, and he used the same method to determine who was the guilty one. The lot indicated it was his own son Jonathan, who was only saved from death by the strongly-expressed will of the people (1 Samuel 14. 36-46). Divination could just as well be used by the enemies of Israel. When the king of Babylon used arrows and entrails for this purpose, Ezekiel knew that the Israelites were destined to fall into their enemy's hand (Ezekiel 21.21). The use of the sacred lot to determine the choice of a candidate lasted at least until the election of Matthias in Acts 1.26.

Mediumship is best illustrated by the story of King Saul at En-Dor (1 Samuel 28). At an earlier stage, he had banished the mediums from the land, but when the sacred lot once more gave him no clear guidance about his strategy for the battle ahead, he went in disguise to 'a woman with a familiar spirit' at En-Dor. At his request, she brought back the departed prophet Samuel, who gave him cold comfort. Saul would go to join Samuel the very next day. At the battle of Mount Gilboa, it all came to pass as it had been foretold.

Visions scatter the pages of the Bible. Some are of angels, as when a fearful servant-boy's eyes are opened to see horses and chariots of fire protecting Elisha from his enemies (2 Kings 6.17).

Some are of the recently-departed, like the appearances of Jesus a few days after his crucifixion. Some are of great figures of the past, as when Moses and Elijah were seen with Jesus by three disciples on the Mount of the Transfiguration (Matthew 17.3). Some are of God himself, as in Isaiah's temple vision (Isaiah 6). There are a good many accounts in the earlier chapters of Genesis where an unusual visitant is subsequently discovered to have been either an angel or God himself (the distinction between them is strangely blurred in the account; see, for example, Genesis 18; 32.1-2; 32.22-30). And angels are frequently of a most terrifying aspect. When Daniel saw a vision of the archangel Gabriel, he prostrated himself face downwards, and the revelation was so unnerving that he lay sick afterwards for several days (Daniel 8.17, 18, 27). St Matthew tells us that the angel who came and rolled away the stone at the tomb of Jesus had a face which shone like lightning, so that the guards shook with fear and fell to the ground as though dead (Matthew 28.3-4). A brush with the supernatural can be an occasion of quite primitive terror.

Voices may be paranormally heard without any visual manifestation. There was one occasion (John 12.27-33) when Jesus was praying and a voice from heaven answered him. Some of the bystanders said that it was thunder; others believed that an angel had spoken to him. Jesus knew that it was a message from his Father.

Xenoglossy or the paranormal acquisition of a foreign language was reported at the Feast of Pentecost (Acts 2.6), when the bystanders could each 'hear in his own native language' what the Galilæan disciples were saying. The phenomenon of 'speaking in tongues' was well-known in the early Church (see Acts 10.46 and 1 Corinthians 14.18), though it is unclear from these later examples whether what was spoken was always an intelligible foreign language or no more than gibberish which had to be subsequently interpreted.

Trance states occur from time to time. The prophet Balaam is described as 'the man whose sight is clear, ... who with opened eyes sees in a trance the vision from the Almighty' (Numbers 24.3-4). He is even credited with being able to hear words spoken by an animal, when his own donkey tells him about the angel barring his way, whom the beast can see, even though it is at first invisible to the prophet (Numbers 22.22-35). And then there is the classic description of a ghostly vision seen by Eliphaz the Temanite (Job 4.13-16):

> In the anxious visions of the night, when everyone sinks into deepest sleep, terror seized me and shuddering; it made my whole frame tremble with fear. A wind brushed across my face and made the hairs of my body stand on end. A figure halted there, whose shape I could not discern, an apparition loomed before me, and I heard a voice murmur.

Healings. Various Old Testament characters were reckoned to have had healing powers, but they all pale into insignificance in comparison with reports of the healings carried out by Jesus of Nazareth. He was able to reverse anything from a fever afflicting a sick old woman (Mark 1.30-31) to the putrefaction of a four-day-old corpse (John 12). The powers seemed to continue into the life of the early Church, when marvellous healings took place, and even handkerchiefs which had been in contact with Paul's skin were discovered to have curative powers (Acts 19.12).

Exorcism. Every writer in the New Testament believed in the existence of evil spirits ill-disposed to the human race, causing illnesses of various kinds, and particularly malevolent towards the Christian God. Their leader was called, variously, Satan, or Beelzebul, or (in the same way that the folk in Harry Potter's world never liked to speak openly about Voldemort, but always called their enemy 'he who must not be named'), they would refer to him as 'the god of this passing age' or 'the commander of the spiritual forces of the air'. Jesus is portrayed as in the front line of the warfare against this demonic enemy, who tried unsuccessfully to tempt him to less than worthy ways of getting people to take notice of his mission. Satan's evil spirits could take charge of people, and there are frequent stories of Jesus commanding them to depart. One poor wretch had a legion of demons troubling him, and Jesus transferred them so effectively to a herd of pigs that they all careered down the hill and drowned in the lake (Luke 8.26-33). Exorcism was not a peculiarly Christian practice. There were plenty of Jewish and pagan practitioners of it as well. Some itinerant exorcists, who had seen how successful Paul was, once tried to cast out an evil spirit in the name of 'Jesus whom Paul proclaims', only to be duffed up by the afflicted man with the words, 'Jesus I know and Paul I know, but who are you?' (Acts 19.13-17).

All these are but samples of the bewildering array of paranormal material with which the pages of the Bible are crowded. What on earth are we to make of them?

#

In these post-modernist days, only the fool-hardy will venture to guess what the original intention of any author was; but when one is dealing with accounts which ostensibly tell of past events, needs must. How many of the incidents I have mentioned so far were intended to be taken literally?

Not all of them, by any means.

The incident of Balaam's speaking ass, for instance (Numbers 22. 22-35). Balaam tried to drive his donkey through a narrow defile and the animal refused to go forward. When Balaam cursed her for her stubbornness, so the story goes, the donkey spoke out and told him why she could get no further. It was because God's angel with a drawn sword was standing in her way. The animal spoke no Hebrew; the account we have was the author's way of saying that Balaam eventually realised what was going on, and that at last he understood why his donkey, on whom he could normally rely so dependably, was taking such an unprecedented liberty with him. Anecdotes about the psychic sensitivity of domesticated animals have been known for thousands of years, and this is an early example of the genre.

Or the coin in the fish's mouth (Matthew 17.27). Peter, the fisherman, had been asked whether Jesus intended to pay the

Temple tax. Jesus told him that he did, and that the next fish Peter caught would have a coin in its mouth, enough to pay for both of them. This was not intended as a prediction of an unusual event. Jesus simply meant that if Peter went about his normal business, he would soon have money enough to pay his dues.

The Biblical writers also knew enough about trickery to unmask it where they needed to. The story in the Apocrypha entitled *Bel and the Dragon* (*Daniel, Bel, and the Snake* in the Revised English Bible) makes Daniel out to be an experienced psychic investigator who was ready to test an apparently paranormal case, to see whether it was due to fraud or not. The great idol Bel stood in a temple which could be securely locked to prevent intrusion. The priests laid out food and drink for him every evening, and by the morning it had all been consumed. King Cyrus was more impressed by this than Daniel was. After the priests had left the temple, the king laid the food out; but Daniel's servants then sifted ashes over the whole place. In the morning, the seals of the temple entrance were intact, but the food was no longer there. Cyrus was ready to believe that the idol had consumed it all, but Daniel showed him the footprints of the priests and their families who had got in through a secret door.

Whether there really was a person called Daniel, whether he was such a psychic sleuth, and whether the incident about Bel ever actually happened, is another matter altogether. Stories about Daniel were a bit like the 'Stories of a Thousand and One Nights'. Daniel was a favourite figure about whom wondrous fictions of a religiously and morally improving nature could be told. When Antiochus Epiphanes was trying to stamp out the practices of Judaism, people needed to be encouraged by patriotic tales of days long ago. We do not need to believe that Daniel was thrown into a burning fiery furnace from which he escaped unscathed; it is sufficient to realise that the story-tellers of the day wanted a narrative which showed how a person who was faithful to his ancestral beliefs was divinely protected from harm. The stories show what people were prepared to believe in (or what stories they could happily listen to with a temporary suspension of disbelief), and were never intended to have much contact with historical accuracy. So we cannot use details from the Daniel stories to prove that particular paranormal incidents took place. The fact that, in the second half of *Daniel, Bel, and the Snake*, the prophet Habakkuk was said to have been lifted up by an angel and carried by the hair from Judæa to Babylon, is (in the words of Pooh-Bah from *The Mikado*) 'merely corroborative detail, intended to give artistic verisimilitude to an otherwise bald and unconvincing narrative'. In each case, we need to establish the literary genre and intentions of the Biblical author before using his text as an account of an apparently paranormal incident.

We do not necessarily have to attribute telepathic powers to Elisha to know how he was able to suss out the battle-plans of the Aramæan king (2 Kings 6.11). He could have had access to good military intelligence. We do not need to attribute telepathic powers to Jesus to explain many of the things people were saying about him. He could have seen Nathanael under the fig-tree (John 1.48) without Nathanael realising he had been observed. He could have known what people were thinking (Matthew 9.4) because he knew their opinions on his actions. That he 'had no need of evidence from others about anyone, for he himself could tell what was in people' (John 2.25) does not necessarily mean that he was acquiring information by telepathy. It could simply mean that he was known to be a shrewd judge of people. We should not assume paranormal influences where none are necessarily involved. (Whether shrewd judges of people are shrewd judges because they are telepathically sensitive as well as sensitive to non-verbal cues or unspoken inferences, is another matter, which needs to be empirically tested. One parapsychological study a number of years ago discovered that successful business executives scored above chance in tests for precognition. That may have been one factor in their ability to choose the best business strategies for their company.)

#

Even if we are satisfied that the authors intended to be taken literally, and that real paranormal events are being alleged, can we believe them? Have the stories, like many contemporary stories we investigate today, grown in the telling? Or been the result of wrong inferences or mal-observation? *Did* Jesus walk on water, or still a storm by a word, or miraculously multiply loaves and fishes, or give sight to the congenitally blind? *Did* he prophesy the manner of his eventual death? *Did* he rise from the dead to leave an empty tomb, and was he seen alive after his burial? Or are these accounts as much fiction as the stories about Daniel?

Attempts at 'explaining away' the miraculous events recorded in the Bible have a long history behind them. Celsus in the second century AD believed the resurrection appearances to be no more than visions of a 'half-frantic woman', and Thomas Woolston issued his *Six Discourses on the Miracles of our Saviour* in 1729, in which he claimed to have proved that the resurrection of Jesus was 'a Piece of Fraud, and his other Miracles to have been all Artifice'. The flood-gates for this type of interpretation opened in earnest in the nineteenth century, with (for example) lives of Jesus by David Friedrich Strauss in 1835 and Ernst Renan in 1863.

All of us are now familiar with interpretations such as that Jesus did not walk on water but was observed paddling near the shore; or that there was no miraculous feeding, but when a young boy started sharing out his packed lunch, all the others who had any food with them were shamed into doing the same. The healing miracles of Jesus have been explained in a number of possible ways. Perhaps they are simply examples of the kind of spontaneous remission of symptoms which all doctors come across from time to time. Or they indicate the power of the placebo, or of psycho-somatic cures. Or the condition was mis-diagnosed, and what was cured was (for example) not leprosy, but dermatitis.

Celsus was certainly not the last commentator to cast doubt on the resurrection narratives. Many people since him have floated alternative theories. Accounts of the resurrection, they said, could have been based on hallucinations born of a fervent and imaginative expectation. Tales of an empty tomb came later, to buttress a belief which had no objective basis. Perhaps Jesus did not die on the Cross, but survived and was spirited away to a life in the South of France where he married Mary Magdalene.

Of course, not all the rationalising explanations are as florid as that, but very many professional Biblical scholars are strangely unwilling to acknowledge that the miraculous events chronicled in the Gospels really happened. Study of the Biblical stories is often guided by what has been termed a 'hermeneutic of suspicion', in which the benefit of any doubt there may be has to count against the historical reliability of the account. People who work on the New Testament documents in this way are at risk, in the graphic words of John Ashton (*The Religion of Paul the Apostle*, p. 168) of being swamped by their own scepticism. With the Gospels in particular, layer after layer of later accretions are stripped off the records, because it is believed that the earliest Christian communities were more likely to be creative than their Lord. The Gospels, so we are told, reflect, not the sayings of the historical Jesus, but the controversies and problems of the early Church. We will never know what Jesus said, whilst what he *did* is even less likely to be discerned.

This intense scepticism has its roots in the unexamined beliefs of the expositors. If you cannot believe that Jesus had flashes of precognition, or even that he was politically astute enough to foretell the eventual end of the Jewish state, you will believe that the Gospel mentions of the fate of Jerusalem must have been added by the evangelists after the city had been sacked by the Romans in AD 70. If, like Rudolf Bultmann more than half a century ago, you hold that 'an historical fact which involves a Resurrection from the dead is utterly inconceivable', you will see the miracles of Jesus as only 'signs and pictures of the Easter faith', and you will think that what we are called to do is not to believe that inconceivable things happened a couple of millennia ago, but to declare that there can be an existential encounter today between God and the naked human soul, in which the preached word of the Gospel faces us with the challenge of the ultimate.

And of course it is important that the word of the Gospel should be preached, and that the human soul should be faced with the challenge of the Ultimate. But it does not follow that there is no objective historical fact on which that challenge is based, or that it is our duty to reject every part of the Gospel record which might possibly have been a later addition to the original sub-stratum.

Such intense historical scepticism is not true historical method. It comes about because some New Testament historians cannot believe that the events with which they are dealing could ever have occurred as reported. They have a very low boggle threshold. The basis on which they refuse to believe is neither scientific nor historical. They are relying, not on science, but on the scientism we encountered in the preceding chapter. That outstanding American parapsychologist, Dr Charles Tart, calls scientism a 'perversion of genuine science' and defines it as 'a dogmatic commitment to a materialist philosophy that "explains away" the spiritual rather than actually examining it carefully and trying to understand it'. Scientism has no time for the data of parapsychology, because it has decided in advance that they cannot happen and that therefore any account of them needs to be explained on materialistic lines. True science takes anomalous phenomena at their face value. It is puzzled by them. It cannot, for the moment, find a satisfactory theoretical framework within which to understand them. But it cannot deny that the data are there.

So a truly scientific historical examination of the Gospel records has to admit that they *might* be accurate records of what happened, and that we cannot deny their historical accuracy simply because they have gone beyond our own personal boggle threshold. We cannot, of course, use the Biblical accounts as part of a proof that paranormal phenomena occur. Standards of proof in parapsychology are very high indeed, and all normal explanations have to be examined and rejected for good reason before a paranormal explanation is considered. So accounts like those in the Bible which have a long oral history behind them, and which have been put into written form many years after the events they describe, are of no use whatever in establishing paranormality. But we are not trying to *prove* that the Biblical accounts are examples of the paranormal. We are simply saying that paranormal events *can* occur, so that the fact that an event described in

Scripture has paranormal aspects to it does not immediately and automatically prevent us from believing that it could have happened as reported.

That is very far from holding a fundamentalist belief that the Gospels are inerrant. We still need to examine the records for consistency, or to see whether, for example, Matthew or Luke have taken over Mark's account of a particular event and subtly altered it to suit their own theological agenda. But we shall be wary of the unexamined presuppositions of so much modern sceptical scholarship, and we may discover that many more of the words and works of Jesus fit into a credible historical frame-work than we had at first imagined possible. As Dr Tom Wright has written in his *Jesus and the Victory of God* (SPCK 1996, pp. 187-8),

> It is prudent, methodologically, to hold back from too hasty a judgment on what is actually possible and what is not within the space-time universe. There are more things in heaven and earth than are dreamed of in post-Enlightenment philosophy. ... To insist at the beginning of an enquiry, whose results (like those of all important enquiries) may call basic worldviews into question, that some particular contemporary worldview is the only possible one, is simply to beg the question, to show that all we really want to do is to hear the echo of our own voices. ... Few serious historians now deny that Jesus, and for that matter many other people, performed cures and did other startling things for which there was no natural explanation.

Paranormal events happen today and they could have happened in the past. We need to hold such a possibility in mind when reading ancient documents like the Bible. That should not prevent us from reading the accounts critically, but we can at least give them as much of the benefit of the doubt as our personal boggle thresholds allow. That does not, of course, give us permission to argue that these things *must* have happened, and they must have happened exactly as the Bible tells us. But it *does* allow us to say, of certain incidents, that if we are to doubt the Bible accounts, we must doubt them on other grounds than that they are impossible. That was the conviction in my own mind more than forty years ago, when I wrote the book entitled *The Easter Enigma* (Faber, 1959). I put forward the hypothesis that the resurrection appearances were similar to present-day crisis apparitions. I am less sure now than I was forty years ago that that suggestion was the correct one; but at least I was making the point that the narratives were a great deal more credible than many people had alleged. People who can get that far towards accepting that the narratives may be trustworthy may still be a long way from believing what Christians believe about the resurrection of Jesus of Nazareth, but they have made a start.

#

Not all Christians think we need to find modern parallels in order to be able to believe the stories we read in the Bible. When God is doing exceptional things like becoming incarnate in human form, they say, we might expect his normal workings to be superseded from time to time. Miracles which do not happen nowadays might well have been appropriate in those exceptional circumstances. At its most extreme, this theology is known as 'dispensationalism'. According to dispensationalists, the history of the world may be divided into various eras or ages or dispensations, and God acts differently, for example, in our own post-Apostolic dispensation from the way in which he worked in New Testament times.

This was a fairly general view in past centuries. For instance, on 5 June 1793, Bishop Samuel Horsley was speaking in the House of Lords about sending ministers of the Gospel to India. He agreed that we ought to make provision for British subjects in that country to attend public worship, but he had very grave doubts indeed about the wisdom of sending missionaries to convert the natives. He did not think that any state had the right to interfere with the government of any other country without an express commission from Heaven. The Apostles had such a commission, and to prove it they were given the power of performing miracles. But that power had now ceased, and the good Bishop believed that the commission of which it was the evidence had ceased with it. Evangelism was alright in AD 93, in the Apostolic dispensation when miracles gave it legitimacy; but it was a very doubtful starter in 1793, when we were in a very different dispensation and miracles no longer happened.

Indeed, if miracles *were* to be observed nowadays, it might mean that Satan was behind them, and was trying to fool us into believing that we were still in an earlier dispensation.

Dispensationalism is no longer main-stream theology, though it is still held by a minority of Christians. Our first reaction to it nowadays might well be to declare that scientists have spent several centuries establishing the fact that the laws of nature are a self-consistent body of observations, and that if any one of them were to cease to apply even for a moment and even in one tiny part of the universe, the knock-on effect everywhere else and for ever after would be unimaginably catastrophic. The regularities of natural law show how God has determined to act in the world he has created, and he has always worked that way. They prove God's care and power better than if he were to intervene in the world in occasional, inconsistent, capricious, and miraculous ways. Scientifically-observed laws of nature hold at all times and in all places, throughout the universe, from the moment of the Big Bang until today. As we sing in a very popular Christian hymn, 'Laws, which *never* shall be broken, For their guidance he hath made'.

That hymn, however, dates from 1796. Since then, our view of nature has had to change. Despite the way in which Einstein used to say that 'God does not play dice', we now know that, at the quantum level, the laws of nature are statistical rather than exact, and that chaos theory can show how a very labile system can be changed out of all recognition by a very slight change at a very great distance - that notorious Beijing butterfly which alters the weather in California. If God has decided to act within the laws of nature which he determined at the moment of the Big Bang, it *may* be that those laws are statistical rather than immutable.

That is a tempting speculation; but we ought not to allow it to run away with us. It is usually over-stated by religious apologists.

Psychical and Spiritual

Events can be indeterminate and probabilistic at a quantum level, and yet they are entirely deterministic at the level at which we normally observe them. The quantum level is more tiny than most people realise, and the probability that indeterminate events could occur at the macroscopic level is unimaginably small, and unlikely to have occurred by chance since the universe began.

All the same, the Laws of Nature, which include the yet-to-be-enunciated laws of parapsychology, could provide for unusual things to have happened around unusual people like Elijah or Elisha or Jesus of Nazareth or Joseph of Copertino or Padre Pio; and unusual people like that do not turn up in every generation. Or perhaps Jesus is more unusual than any other human being and the incarnation of God as man adds so much to what is possible for normal human nature that the possibilities are limitless, ranging from control of the weather to the multiplication of food, or from the bringing back to life of a dead body to a physical resurrection and an empty tomb. But we are moving here from parapsychological speculation to theological speculation, which may be devotionally helpful, but is not likely to be very scientifically profitable. Let us for the moment be content with the conclusion that we will still need to have our critical faculties at the alert when we are studying our Bibles, and we shall be well advised to ask whether a piece of narrative is intended as a parable, a myth, an improving fiction, or a piece of history: but we may be less likely to reject a Biblical narrative as literal truth if we have a working knowledge of the parapsychological possibilities that exist in this amazing world of ours.

#

What does the Bible say about the exercise of psychic gifts? I used to live just across the road from Cranmer Hall theological college. Every year it puts on a special course for its students in order to prepare them to cope with questions about dying, death, and bereavement which they are likely to come across as Christian ministers. For several years before my retirement, I used to do a morning on this course with the title *Contact with the*

Departed? (the question mark was very deliberate). I dealt with the questions of whether the departed can (or do) contact us, and whether we can (or ought to try to) contact them. It was always a lively morning's teaching; and since most Cranmer Hall students are Evangelicals with a very properly high doctrine of the importance of Holy Scripture, the conservatives usually came out of the woodwork sooner or later, to ask how I could justify even having an interest in this subject when the Bible condemns it so strongly.

Leviticus 19.31, for example. 'Do not turn to mediums or wizards; do not seek them out, to be defiled with them'. Or Deuteronomy 18.9-14, which tells the Israelites that when they come into the Promised Land they must not follow any of the 'abominable practices' of the people who live there, such as practising divination, or being a soothsayer, or an augur, or a sorcerer, or a charmer, or a medium, or a necromancer. 'Whoever does these things is an abomination to the Lord'. Or Isaiah 8.19-20, where the people of God are being tempted to 'consult the mediums and the wizards who chirp and mutter', and the prophet answers that they should, rather, consult their God. It is, he says, ridiculous that they should consult the dead on behalf of the living.

How did I reply to that sort of accusation?

It is hard to escape the feeling that in some degree at any rate, the pot is calling the kettle black. Moses and Aaron could do magic tricks even better than those performed by the magicians of Pharaoh. Daniel was an interpreter of dreams and visions as much as the Chaldæans. For all the Biblical authors' inveighing against divination and augury, we have seen that it was common within Israelite religion itself, and practised by Joseph and Saul; and the great prophets like Elijah and Elisha were portrayed as having quite amazingly developed psychic gifts. Perhaps it is the case that if these gifts are exercised in the cause of Jahwistic religion, they are legitimate, but if they are linked to Canaanite practices, they have to be condemned.

The test case, however, is not the practice of divination, but recourse to 'people with familiar spirits' who claim to make contact with the dead. Why was this regarded by the Old Testament writers as particularly heinous? And should we be bound by their prohibitions?

It is certainly true that many of the Old Testament prohibitions no longer have any force for Christians. That same nineteenth chapter of Leviticus, for instance, which tells us not to turn to mediums or wizards, also forbids us to wear a garment woven with two kinds of cloth or to shave the edges of our beards. If we are free to disregard one set of prohibitions, why get so uptight about another, in an adjacent verse of the same document?

The trouble with that kind of approach is that it proves too much. There must be some interpretative standard. We cannot simply allow ourselves to pick and choose at random, and laugh out of court anything that we find inconvenient; that would be tantamount to saying that Scripture had no objective moral authority. We need, instead, to have some criteria to judge which laws were of temporary relevance and which are of permanent validity.

The laws in the Old Testament are of three kinds. Some are moral laws of binding permanence. Some are ritual regulations which have been superseded. But some do not apply any longer because a theological insight has been developed in the course of the Biblical revelation which has led us to alter our attitude towards the matter in hand. For an example of this third category, look at the final two chapters of the book of Ezra. Those Israelites who had married foreign wives were forced to put them away. To Ezra, this was a way of showing that, at whatever cost in terms of personal heartache, the purity of Israelite religion and culture needed to be maintained. We do not see it at all in that way. To us, it looks like a particularly revolting example of ethnic cleansing. Our moral insights have developed since the time of Ezra.

I believe that the prohibition against mediumship is another example of this third kind of Old Testament law. It was part of an attempt to maintain the purity of Israelite religion at a time when it was in danger of being swamped by the beliefs of the surrounding nations.

The constant temptation of the average Israelite was to jettison the religion of their own nation and adopt the religious practices of their non-Israelite contemporaries. Sometimes, of course, that temptation was not resisted, and it led to an enrichment of Israelite religion. That was especially true when Persian ideas and practices entered the cult during and after the Exile. But there were times when to do this would have led to an impoverishment of what was distinctively Israelite, and then it was strenuously opposed by prophet and priest, whose teachings were eventually codified in the books which became our Old Testament.

The degree to which such opposition was expressed differed from age to age, and there is an interesting example of this in the familiar story of the time when King Saul consulted a psychic sensitive. After the death of Samuel, on whom he had relied so much, Saul was faced with a decisive battle against the Philistines. He tried to get guidance from the sacred divination by the Urim and Thummim, but no reply was forthcoming. He had at an earlier stage cast the psychic sensitives out of his kingdom, but he discovered one at En-Dor and asked her to bring Samuel back so he could ask him what to do.

There are two reports of the consultation. One is in 1 Samuel 28, which may go back to an almost contemporary account, and the other can be found in 1 Chronicles 10, within an account of Israelite history compiled several centuries later. In 1 Samuel, the woman is presented in a very positive light. She risks her life to help Saul (who visits her incognito), and when the séance is over, and she sees he is tired and hungry, she slaughters her own fatted calf to provide a meal for him and his companions. The shade of Samuel tells Saul that God has deserted him. It was, however, not for any sin of psychic trafficking. His fault was that he had not been thorough enough in exterminating his Amalekite enemies. Compare all that with the account in 1 Chronicles, and we see that the later writer has interpreted the whole incident as an example of the wickedness of Saul, who 'paid with his life for his unfaithfulness: he had disobeyed the word of the LORD and had resorted to ghosts for guidance'.

Why was it thought that Israelite religion would be fatally compromised if mediumistic activity was permitted? It was because the people of the land which the Hebrews took over had a lively sense of the commerce that was possible between this world and the world to which we come at our death. Israelite religion, on the other hand, had a very shadowy conception of this Next World, and believed that the writ of Jahweh did not run there. Sheol, the place of the departed, was a grey land inhabited by powerless shades. So the prophet Isaiah (14.9-11) taunts the king of Babylon, who on his death has become entirely powerless. Like all the leaders on earth who have gone to Sheol, he is now absolutely impotent. On earth, he may have been used to luxury, but now, maggots are his mattress and worms his coverlet.

Similarly, the Psalmist complains that in his despair he has 'become like a man beyond help, abandoned among the dead', and he knows that those who lie in the grave are held in mind no more, because they are cut off from God's care (Psalm 88.4-5), that 'the dead praise not thee, O Lord : neither all they that go down into silence' (Ps. 115.17), and that 'When the breath of man goeth forth he shall turn again to his earth : and then all his thoughts perish' (Ps. 146.3).

That was why mediumship was so suspect. If the writ of Israel's God did not extend to the realm of the dead, then it was disloyalty to Jahweh to consult the departed. Those who did so, were seeking guidance from a spiritual source over which Jahweh had no control.

This ancient Israelite conviction that Jahweh was a God of this world only, lasted for a very long time. Only in a few texts, and those from the latest part of the Old Testament (like the 'Thou art there also' of Psalm 139.8), is there any suggestion that Jahweh's kingdom could extend beyond this earth. Eventually the old doctrine began to be questioned, but not until the slaughter of the faithful in the Maccabæan wars of the second century BC. Then some Israelite religious thinkers began to toy with the idea that those who had died for the preservation of their ancestral faith might be rewarded by Jahweh in a life with him beyond this earth.

By the time of Jesus of Nazareth, this was the subject of lively theological debate, but there was as yet no agreement about it. The Sadducees denied that there was any resurrection, or angel, or spirit; but the Pharisees believed in all three (as we see from the comment in Acts 23.8).

The resurrection of Jesus blew this whole controversy apart. If it was true that God was in Christ (2 Corinthians 5.19), then when Jesus died, God became present to the world of the departed (1 Peter 3,19; 4.6 - what the mediævals called the 'harrowing of hell'). There is now no place where God is not. Christians know that when they are contacting the departed, they are not going off God's territorial limits. They can do so without being disloyal to him.

The full implications of this did not immediately dawn on the young Church. Indeed, it has not dawned on some Christians even now. Attitudes moulded over centuries take centuries to be re-formed. But, as a result of the death and resurrection of our God and Christ, we are now set free, as the people of the Old Testament were not, to be discriminating.

And discrimination is necessary. Not everyone has the discretion to use their psychic gifts wisely. When Jesus cured people who had been obsessed by evil spirits, he sometimes had to tell them not to publicise the fact, because the way in which they would have done so would have detracted from the value of his message. When Paul found a slave-girl with an oracular spirit at Philippi, he saw that she was so obsessive about the gift which her owners were prostituting that she had to be completely wrenched away from it (Acts 16.18). The Bible rightly warns us that there are dangers in psychism: but there is opportunity as well as danger.

Committed Christians need to develop a positive and healthy theology of psychic sensitivity, so that it can be a means of leading people away from darkness and error into the light of the knowledge and service of the true God in the face of Jesus Christ. There are, sadly, many ways of using psychic sensitivity which pander to human self-centredness rather than to a mature trust in the living God whose gift that sensitivity is. *That* is the true parallel to the Biblical prohibitions of psychic activity. If our psychism prevents people from seeing that true human fulfilment is only to be found in the whole-hearted service of the One True God, it needs to be strenuously eschewed. Sadly, that is what happens in so much popular Spiritualism. We can only safely use any of our human powers if we use them to the greater glory of God and the true service of our fellow-creatures.

That, however, is too large a subject for the tail-end of a study of the Biblical witness. We will return to it in greater detail in our final chapter.

4

From the realms of glory

From earliest recorded times, there have been accounts of men and women who have claimed to see events, things, and beings not visible to the eyes of more 'normal' people. What are these visionaries seeing? The deluded fantasies of their own over-active imaginations? The results of psychedelic chemicals in their blood-streams? The florid hallucinations of a schizophrenic mind?

Sometimes, yes. But psychotic and drug-induced hallucinations are frequently bizarre, terrifying, and irrational. There are other types of visionary experience which, though they may be terrifying, cannot be categorised in that way. In these cases, has the visionary been vouchsafed an awareness of strange realities which are normally hidden from most of the rest of us? Let us look at a few examples. Some of these accounts have been handed down in sacred writings of old; some of them are experiences of our contemporaries. They are accounts of what we call 'religious experiences', and they occur in a wide variety of contexts.

For instance. Around the end of the first Christian century, there was a man who wished to encourage his fellow-believers by writing down what he had seen (in a trance? in a reverie? in a dream?) whilst he was on the Greek island of Patmos.

> At once the Spirit came upon me. There in heaven stood a throne. On it sat One whose appearance was like jasper or cornelian, and round about it was a rainbow, bright as an emerald. As I looked I heard, all round the throne and the living creatures and the elders, the voices of many angels, thousands on thousands, myriads on

myriads. They proclaimed with loud voices: 'Worthy is the Lamb who was slain, to receive power and wealth, wisdom and might, honour and glory and praise!' The four living creatures said, 'Amen', and the elders prostrated themselves in worship (Rev. 4. 2-3; 5.11-12, 14).

But that was nineteen hundred years ago, in the Bible. We may think that things like that no longer happen nowadays, and certainly not to people like us. But we may be mistaken.

The following account can be found in Raynor Johnson's marvellous book *The Imprisoned Splendour*, which was first published by Hodder and Stoughton fifty years ago. Johnson abridged it from a volume entitled *Contemplations* by W.L. Wilmshurst, and I have shortened it even further for our present purposes, but the longer account on pages 306-7 of Johnson's book is well worth consulting. Ever since I first read it, it has stayed with me as a marvellous account of a profound religious experience.

It happened at morning prayer, in an English village church, in the early years of the twentieth century, before the Parish Eucharist had supplanted Morning Prayer as the staple diet of Anglican worshippers. The choir was beginning to sing the *Te Deum*. Let us take up what then happened to a member of the congregation, in his own words:

> My thought began to contrast the modest praises uttered in this humble place in the outward world, by its crippled organ, the puny voices of the juvenile choir and handful of villagers with the stupendous unimaginable paeans which must needs be heard above. Whilst thus reflecting I caught sight, in the aisle at my side, of what resembled bluish smoke issuing from the chinks of the stone floor, as though from fire smouldering beneath. Looking more intently I saw it was not smoke, but something finer, more tenuous - a soft impalpable self-luminous haze of violet colour, unlike any physical vapour. Upon the instant the luminous blue haze engulfing me and all around me became transformed into golden glory, into light untellable. But the most wonderful thing was that these shafts and waves of light, that vast expanse of photosphere, and even the central globe itself, were crowded to solidarity with the forms of

living creatures. I saw moreover that these beings were present in teeming myriads in the church I stood in. The heavenly hosts drifted through the human congregation as wind passes through a grove of trees; beings of radiant beauty and clothed in shimmering raiment.

As that vision faded, the worshipper found himself still standing in the church, well and physically unmoved, and discovered that no-one else had been aware of what had happened to him.

Only a few moments [he wrote] could have been occupied by an experience in the spirit, of which the incidents were so vivid and the details so numerous that my memory still fails to exhaust them. The singing of the 'Te Deum' had not concluded.

What are we to make of that? Was it an objective vision of the heavenly host, or was it a subjective experience of a worshipper who had an over-developed visual imagination? For that matter, was St John on Patmos simply writing an uplifting piece of fiction to encourage persecuted Christians, or was he having self-induced mystical visions, or was he seeing something which actually existed?

According to the Bible and the Collect of Michaelmas Day in the Book of Common Prayer, God's holy angels exist, and they 'alway do him service in heaven'. But is that true? And, if it is, can anybody on earth ever see what is going on in heaven? Are the psychics and the mystics and the visionaries tapping into anything *real*?

Before we think of answering this question, we need to look at some of the other claims that are made about angels and their activities. That same Collect of Michaelmas Day which states that the angels do God service in heaven also asks that they may succour and defend us here on earth; and there are modern as well as ancient accounts which claim that they still do so. Let us look at one Biblical and one contemporary account of the help which angels are alleged to bring to us incarnate humans.

The first story comes from chapter 12 of the book of the Acts of the Apostles. Peter had been imprisoned by King Herod and was held under guard, awaiting his examination and trial. The account continues:

> On the very night before Herod had planned to produce him, Peter was asleep between two soldiers, secured by two chains, while outside the doors sentries kept guard over the prison. All at once an angel of the Lord stood there, and the cell was ablaze with light. He tapped Peter on the shoulder to wake him. 'Quick! Get up!', he said, and the chains fell away from Peter's wrists. The angel said, 'Do up your belt and put on your sandals.' He did so. 'Now wrap your cloak round you and follow me.' Peter followed him out, with no idea that the angel's intervention was real; he thought it was just a vision. They passed the first guard-door, then the second, and reached the iron gate leading out into the city. This opened for them of its own accord; they came out and had walked the length of one street when suddenly the angel left him.
>
> Then Peter came to himself. 'Now I know it is true', he said: 'the Lord has sent his angel and rescued me.'

It is possible to think of that incident as something which was recorded thousands of years ago, and in the Bible, and to believe that things like that do not happen today. But we may be mistaken.

A few years ago, a lady called Joan Anderson had a son who lived in Arizona. One winter, he was marooned in his car in a blizzard. When he thought that he was stuck there for the night, and that his life might well be in danger in that intense cold, all of a sudden a tow-truck turned up, hitched itself to his immobile vehicle, and got him safely home. The truck and its driver made off without waiting to be thanked. When Joan's son saw that its wheels made no tracks in the virgin snow, he knew that it was no human that had got him out of trouble.

As a lifelong student of parapsychology, I know how so many stories like this evaporate on closer examination. We only have Joan Anderson's word for what her son told her. Were there independent witnesses? Did anyone interview Joan's son immediately after the event in order to make sure he had got the details right? Or was it, as so many stories like this prove to be when they are more closely examined, a tale which has grown taller with every telling? Observation is notoriously inaccurate. Memory is so fallible. It seems impossible to get watertight evidence that anything paranormal has ever taken place. What really happened? Was it a supernatural visitation? Or was it just that someone came and helped, and did not want the fuss of being thanked? And the snow was drifting so fast that by the time Joan's son looked out again, there was no sign of wheel-marks?

For that matter, what happened to St Peter? Did a Christian helper get hold of a set of keys and rescue him, and the story just grew in the telling? We shall never know for certain.

Etymologically, the word 'angel' means 'messenger', and there are scores of occasions in the Bible which illustrate the activity of angels as message-bearers. For instance, here is a story about the prophet Elisha, but I am not sure which category to put it in. It could be classed as a message, assuring the person who had the experience that God was in charge; or perhaps it was a narrative about actual help given to the prophet by the angelic hosts.

Elisha, that noted psychic (2 Kings 6), confounded the Aramæan king by telling the King of Israel the things that his enemy was saying in his secret counsels. The King of Aram did not like it, and sent a troop of men with horses and chariots to surround the town. The next morning, Elisha's servant lad saw the troops and cried out in dismay, 'O master; which way are we to turn?' Elisha answered, 'Do not be afraid, for those who are on our side are more than those who are on theirs'; then continued, 'O Lord, open the eyes of this young man, that he may see'. And the Lord opened the eyes of the young man and he saw the whole hill swarming with horses and chariots of fire round about Elisha.

As I say, that could be classed as a message that God was in charge; or it could be classed as help given to Elisha and his servant when they most needed it. There are plenty of stories in the Bible about God sending his messages to human beings, and using angels to do it. Many of the apocalyptic passages in the Bible tell of visions which are meaningless to the visionary until their interpretation has been revealed by an angel (see, for example, Zechariah 1.9, or Revelation 22.6). Other messages are more straightforward. The one that will come most readily to the mind of the majority is the message Gabriel brought to Mary:

> In the sixth month the angel Gabriel was sent by God to Nazareth, a town in Galilee, with a message for a girl betrothed to a man named Joseph, a descendant of David; the girl's name was Mary. ... The angel said to her, 'Do not be afraid, Mary, for God has been gracious to you; you will conceive and give birth to a son, and you are to give him the name Jesus.'

But, again, even if we say it was possible for a thing like that to happen, it still happened a very long time ago and only in an ancient sacred book. Do things like that still happen today? Do we still get messages from God through his angels?

I am sure we all know of times when we have received messages of spiritual importance to us. Perhaps we attribute them to the inspiration of our own hidden human potential; but perhaps we might be allowed to believe that those moments of insight have come to us because an angel has communicated with us. Certainly many of the great musicians and the great artists and the great writers have acknowledged that their work has been possible, not because they had such marvellous ideas, but because they simply took down what they heard or saw from a source which seemed to be outside them. Socrates called that source his *dæmon*. Christians would call it an angel of the God who is the source of all truth and beauty, both moral and aesthetic.

Some messages from God come by paranormal (supernatural) means, and some come perfectly naturally. Some of them are welcome messages, whilst others are distinctly unwelcome. Sometimes, messages from God need to be bad news before they can be good news. There is a mysterious line in T.S. Eliot's *Murder in the Cathedral* where Archbishop Thomas à Becket is waiting for the assassins to come and murder him, and he prays,

> Now my good angel, whom God appoints
> To be my guardian, hover over the swords' points.

What does that mean? Does it simply mean that Becket is asking his guardian angel to prevent his enemies' swords from piercing his flesh? I think (if I have the right reading) that it is something a little deeper than that, and that Eliot wanted us to realise that God may bring good out of evil, and our *good* angels may hover over us whilst *bad* things are happening to us; in order to bring good out of them.

#

So many of the popular stories about angels which fill book after book today (and there are an immense number of them) domesticate the numinous and turn the ineffable into a cosy fireside encounter. If angels really exist, they are otherworldly, supernatural, beings, and if we were to be vouchsafed a vision of one, we would more likely be terrified than consumed with curiosity.

When Daniel had a vision of the archangel Gabriel, he prostrated himself in terror, face downwards; and the revelation to him was so disturbing that he lay sick afterwards for several days (Daniel 8. 17-18, 27). When the guards at the grave of Jesus saw the angel who came and rolled away the stone, he had a face which shone like lightning, so that at the sight of him they shook with fear and became as dead men (Matt. 28. 3-4). Daniel, of course, as was mentioned in the last chapter, is more likely a fictional tale than an historical record, and Matthew's account can hardly have come first-hand from the only people who, he tells us, witnessed this incident; but the point here is that both these authors warn us away from treating angels lightly. We have seen so many twee representations of them in kitsch art that we find it hard to imagine just how awesome it would be if we were to see one of them as they really are.

But how do we know what angels look like? That is an impossible question, because angels are part of the world which is unseen and therefore they do not appear to our physical eyes. When we have an apprehension of the supernatural, we may clothe it in images which make sense for us. Though those images may be the conventional images of angels as young women with wings, playing on harps, they can just as easily be images of very different kinds, such as luminous beings in heavenly glory, or very ordinary beings who look for all the world like truck drivers.

Angels can certainly take on a very plain appearance. Sometimes, people have come across angels unawares. At first, they seemed humdrum, but then they did something which revealed their true nature, and the person who was having the experience suddenly came to the numinous realisation that what had seemed so much a part of this ordinary earth was in fact a being of another order altogether.

Some of the stories about angelic appearances in the early chapters of the book Genesis in the Old Testament have that characteristic. They may tell us about events which are alleged to have happened at the very dawn of the human race, and the accounts as we have them certainly have a long written and oral prehistory; but that does not stop them from being able to tell us some revealing things about that part of God's creation which usually remains unseen by us humans, and the surprisingly human appearance which the angels may initially present.

> By the terebinths of Mamre [we are told in Genesis 18], as Abraham was sitting at the opening of his tent in the heat of the day, he looked up and saw three men standing over against him. On seeing them, he hurried from his tent door to meet them. Bowing low, he said, 'Sirs, if I have deserved your favour, do not go past your servant without a visit. Let me send for some water so that you may bathe your feet; and rest under this tree, while I fetch a little food so that you may refresh yourselves. Afterwards you may continue the journey which has brought you my way.' They said, 'Very well, do as you say.'

The story continues. Abraham sets the best of his food before the three visitors and waits on them himself. They ask him about his wife Sarah, and promise her a son. Sarah, listening at the opening of the tent, laughs to herself, because she knows she is past the age for child-bearing. But then there is a sudden and unnerving change of gear in the account. 'The LORD said to Abraham, "Why did Sarah laugh? Is anything impossible for the LORD?" '

Why do we change suddenly from three visitors who might be any group of wandering Bedouin, and suddenly find that God is brought into the story? It was because they were no ordinary visitors. Indeed, we were told so at the beginning of the story, and the selective way in which those verses from Genesis were printed a couple of paragraphs ago was deliberately misleading in a way which the account which has come down to us certainly was not. It did not begin with the words 'By the terebinths of Mamre'. It began, *'The LORD appeared to Abraham* by the terebinths of Mamre'. The author wants us to know at the outset of his story that what he is describing was not an appearance of three Bedouin travellers, but an epiphany of God himself. And when Sarah laughed at the impossibility of the promise, it was God himself who asked whether there was anything too impossible for him to do.

But, at any rate for the writers of the Old Testament, God is God and all alone and evermore shall be so. In the fifteenth Christian century, the Russian orthodox icon painter Andrei Rublev could transform Abraham's three visitors into an Old Testament foreshadowing of God the Holy Trinity, but that was not what the writer of Genesis intended us to see. The Lord can only be one of the visitors. Who are the others?

As the story goes on, the answer to that question becomes clear. The visitors set out and go towards Sodom, and Abraham goes with them to see them on their way. Then the Lord decides to make Abraham privy to his intentions for that wicked city. He will destroy it, because there are not enough righteous men in it to make it worth saving. Abraham tries to beat him down, and in the end the Lord agrees that if as few as ten righteous men (the quorum for a synagogue in later Judaism) were to be found in the place, he could spare it. Alas, as the reader is soon to discover, that was not to be.

So 'when the LORD had finished talking to Abraham, he went away, and Abraham returned home', but 'the two angels' went on, and got as far as Sodom by evening.

'The two angels'! Now we have been let into the secret of who they were. Did Abraham know *that*, when he first saw three travellers approaching his settlement? Did Lot know who those two characters were, when they came to his house and spent the night there? Did the people of Sodom know, when they thumped on Lot's door that night and demanded to abuse the two visitors? Angels do not always announce themselves by appearing in their true and numinous guise. 'Do not neglect to show hospitality', we read in the Letter to Hebrews (13.2); 'by doing this, some have entertained angels unawares'. Unawares we can put ourselves in the way of a blessing, as Abraham did; a blessing for himself and all future generations, as he received his beloved son Isaac, 'Laughter' - named for that incident in which his super-human guests made him so incredible a promise that at first it was simply laughed at. Unawares we can put ourselves in for disaster, as the men of Sodom did. They thought they were simply harassing a couple of strangers in their midst, but those strangers were no ordinary visitors.

Angels unawares. We seem to move, in these Genesis accounts, from human figures to figures of angels and to the figure of God himself, in ways which defy the logic of any story. Figures that begin by looking very human and very ordinary, suddenly glow with the mystery of a numinous reality, as we see that things on this earth are not always things of this earth.

In the earliest times, people who had this kind of numinous awareness spoke of it as a direct interaction with God himself, who could be seen and touched, and who could come and eat at a human's table; but who would not reveal his Name except to those who had proved worthy of that honour.

That is part of the message of that strange tale of what happened to Jacob at the ford of the Jabbok one fateful night. Jacob had cheated his elder brother Esau of his birthright and had to flee for his life. He took sanctuary with his cousin Laban until Esau's anger had had time to die down. By a mixture of good luck and sharp practice he made himself rich at Laban's expense, and, by then, thought it might be time to make up the family feud. In the hopes that it might ingratiate him, he sent a sumptuous set of gifts ahead of him. But now it was the day before the fateful meeting. Jacob must have been anxious. Was he as safe as he hoped he might be? By the evening, he had got as far as the ford of the Jabbok and the camp had settled down for the night.

> During the night Jacob rose, and taking his two wives, his two slave-girls, and his eleven sons, he crossed the ford of Jabbok. After he had sent them across the wadi with all that he had, Jacob was left alone, and a man wrestled with him there till daybreak. When the man saw that he could not get the better of Jacob, he struck him in the hollow of the thigh, so that Jacob's hip was dislocated as they wrestled. The man said, 'Let me go, for the day is breaking,' but Jacob replied, 'I will not let you go unless you bless me.' The man asked, 'What is your name?' 'Jacob,' he answered. The man said, 'Your name shall no longer be Jacob but Israel, because you have striven with God and with mortals, and have prevailed.' Jacob said, 'Tell me *your* name, I pray.' He replied, 'Why do you ask my name?' but he gave him his blessing there. Jacob called the place Peniel, 'because', he said, 'I have seen God face to face yet my life is spared'. The sun rose as Jacob passed through Penuel, limping because of his hip (Gen. 32. 22-31).

Jacob wanted a blessing, but he wanted it on terms which included his knowing the Name; being in control of what was going on between God and himself. It had to be the other way round. God needed to control Jacob. But God was gracious. Although his reply to Jacob's demand was 'Why do you ask my Name?', still he gave him his blessing there. And Jacob acknowledged that he had seen God face to face, yet his life was spared.

The writer of Genesis tells us that the divine assailant did, in fact, reveal his Name to Jacob, but only at a later stage. After he had been reconciled with Esau, whom he had so badly wronged, Jacob settled in Shechem. Then God said to him, 'Go to Beth-El and set up an altar there'. Jacob set off to that place, where he had long ago seen in his dream a vision of angels going up and down a ladder between earth and heaven. But there was something else to be done first. He made sure he and his whole company got rid of all their foreign gods before they set out. When he had proved his loyalty to God by doing this and by building the new altar, then, and only then, did God appear to him once more and reveal the divine Name of El Shaddai - God Almighty (Genesis 35. 1-11). God does not reveal his Name to us on demand, but only when we prove our loyalty to him by what we do.

The people who recorded sacred encounters like this, and who pondered them in their hearts, had to try and make sense of them. Did the ancients see God and wrestle with him? Did he come to their tents and eat with them? Gradually, as the immensity of God dawned on the people of Israel, they began to think that it could not possibly have been God himself whom they saw; no human could see him and live. It must have been some supernatural being whose nature lay between divinity and humanity - an angel. But the traces of the older belief were never entirely expunged from the stories as they were told and re-told and eventually committed to writing.

And if the ancients had been favoured with a vision of a supernatural being, they gradually came to the conviction that that being could not possibly have done anything so crass as to have eaten and drunk the materials of human nourishment. So the eating and drinking gets removed from the story; but, again, not entirely, so that we can still read that Abraham's three visitors ate at his table and (presumably) at Lot's when they stayed the night with him in Sodom. But in a comparable story in Judges 13, it is explicitly denied that the angel ever partook of the food that was laid before him:

> Manoah said to the angel of the LORD, 'May we urge you to stay? Let us prepare a young goat for you.' The angel replied, 'Though you urge me to stay, I shall not eat your food; but prepare a whole-offering if you will, and offer that to the LORD.'... Manoah took a young goat with the proper grain-offering, and offered it on the rock to the LORD, to him whose works are full of wonder. While Manoah and his wife were watching, the flame went up from the altar towards heaven, and the angel of the LORD ascended in the flame (Judges 13. 15-16, 19-20).

Here again, (as so often in these Old Testament stories which have been worked over for generations before being frozen into written form) there are traces of an older narrative, in which it was not an angel, but God who appeared to Manoah and his wife. 'We are doomed to die', they said, 'for we have seen God', but they are spared, and Manoah's wife bears a child, whom they name Samson and who turns out to be a mighty (though morally flawed) warrior for God.

But whether it was God or his angel, the final author makes clear that it was a supernatural being and therefore not one who could take nourishment fit only for earthly creatures. Similarly, in the (much later) tale of Tobias and the angel, when Raphael reveals his true identity, he is careful to say, 'Take note that I ate no food' (Tobit 12.19). That is why St Luke is adamant to point out that the risen Jesus ate and drank with his followers, to prove that he was no ghost or spirit (Luke 24.36-43).

#

We are already in the dangerous area of deciding what angels can and cannot do, and it is only a short step from there to the even more hazardous procedure of trying to comprehend the angelic hosts by codifying them, classifying them and giving them name, rank, and number.

That final step was taken by a writer who wrote under the pseudonym of Dionysius. The real Dionysius was an Athenian member of the court of Areopagus whom we come across in Acts 17.34, but the person who took his name was from Syria, a mystical writer of the sixth Christian century. He arranged the supernatural beings in three hierarchies of three choirs each: Seraphim, Cherubim, and Thrones; Dominions, Virtues, and Powers; and Principalities, Archangels and Angels. The first seven are engaged in purely heavenly activities, and only the last two can appear on earth or be concerned with human affairs.

We should never under-estimate the depth of the mystical experience of Dionysius, but we should begin to be suspicious when he tells us so much about the heavenly realms. The same is true of Emanuel Swedenborg, that eighteenth-century Swedish scientist and mystic, who had an almost daily experience of angels and the spiritual world in dreams and visions, as well as in his normal waking life. He described heaven and hell, their mysteries and their inhabitants, in great detail.

How far the writings of Dionysius and Swedenborg give us objective descriptions of places, states, and beings which they had seen, and how far they are human attempts at giving concrete and visual content to an essentially inner mystical experience, is the important question. My own inclination is to regard them as left-hemisphere descriptions of right-hemisphere experiences. The logical and verbal expression of left-hemisphere analysis is inadequate to describe the kind of experiences which come through the brain's right hemisphere and, as we have seen, may be evoked but cannot ever be described.

It is a common human failing to try and package and label the ineffable instead of simply recognising that it cannot be confined within any concrete system or categorisation. What we can name and systematise, we are in danger of believing we understand, and even of believing we can make use of it for our own purposes, and of imagining we might be able to control it.

Names are strange things. If we are not careful, we will say that when people have visions of angels, it is another way of saying that they have had a 'religious experience'. And that is a very dangerous thing to say, because if there is something we do not understand, and we put a name on it, we pretend that that makes us understand it. And understanding is only one step away from saying it was 'only' what we named it to be. Very often (and particularly in religion and in parapsychology, and, so psychiatrists tell me, in psychiatry too) a name is simply a way of cloaking our ignorance. When we come across something paranormal, and we call it an example of 'telepathy' or 'clairvoyance', we may feel a bit happier about it, but we do not thereby understand it any the better, any more than we understand a haunting by calling it a 'place memory'. No more would Jacob have understood what happened to him at Jabbok if his mysterious assailant had answered his demand for a Name. Naming implies control, and we cannot control the numinous. It (or should it be 'he'?) has to control us.

What, then, are we aware of, when we are aware of the angels of God around us, protecting us or showing us the way to go? Just because the experience of an angel is a right-hemisphere thing, belonging to the realm of emotion or numinous awareness, there is no reason why it should not possess an objective reality. If religious experience can be the experience of an objective God and not simply a way of fooling ourselves, so can the awareness of angels.

At the time of Jesus, there were Pharisees and Sadducees. We are told that 'the Saducees deny that there is any resurrection or angel or spirit, but the Pharisees believe in all three' (Acts 23.8). I feel sorry for the Sadducees. We know that the angels keep their ancient places and that we have sometimes only to turn a stone to start a wing. The Sadducees, with their thin rationalistic materialism that estranged their faces, missed the many-splendoured things that lay around them.

And so do so many people today. They are so earthly minded that they are no heavenly use. For them, St Michael is not the captain of the heavenly host, but the guardian angel of Marks and Spencers; the patron saint of mass-produced underwear. A few years ago, Malcolm Godwin wrote a book entitled *Angels - An Endangered Species* (Newleaf, 1995). Angels would only be endangered if they were like fairies in *Peter Pan*, which ceased to exist if people stopped believing in them. But, thank God, they are not like that. They do not depend on us for their existence. They are not an endangered species; they are all around us. We simply need to have our eyes opened to them, like Elisha's servant boy about whom we were reminded a few pages back.

And where are they? The most satisfactory thing to say is that they are in their own space, or the space of heaven, or of one of the heavens. That space normally does not interact with our space, but on the occasions when it does, we can become aware of it. Science today is familiar with the idea of there being more than one space, and of discrete spaces which do not interact with each other. Atomic scientists nowadays are quite ready to talk about particles which can never be detected by the equipment they have in their laboratories, because they do not interact with any other particles. Only particles which have an effect on other particles can be detected by the instruments which the scientists have constructed. Similarly, we are normally only aware of things in our four-dimensional universe if they interact with the material particles of our bodies, and in particular with the material structure of our brains, which are marvellously constructed so as to turn thought or consciousness into physical or electrical impulses. Only when particles interact with the material components of our scientific equipment can we detect their presence, or can our brains become conscious of them. It may be that the bodies of the angels are made up of the kind of particles which do not interact with the material particles of our physical world, so that we are usually completely unaware of the fact that they are occupying space.

Particles; or something else? We know that mass and energy are inter-convertible, that energy is carried in wave motions, and that the building-blocks of the universe can be described either as particles or as waves, according to the way we are trying to perceive them. As we have already noted, it is perfectly possible for many waves to coexist in the same space. Myriads of radio, television, mobile phone, and radar waves all pass through the same space that our bodies are occupying without our having the faintest inkling of their existence or of the messages that they are carrying. But when there is a suitably-tuned receiver, the message can come into consciousness.

It is therefore quite compatible with modern science to believe that our minds are tuned so that they can (but only on occasion and not as a regular thing) be aware of angelic presences. Exceptional minds, like that of Emanuel Swedenborg, can be more often aware of them than the rest of us, and we have to take their word for it when they tell us what they are seeing, even though it is something that we are unable to perceive. But the total creation of God is many-splendoured and beyond our wildest dreams.

From the realms of glory

Why should we not believe in angels? Why should not the voice of conscience be the result of messages received from an angelic source? Why should not the way in which some teaching about God strikes us with a particular freshness at some particular time be because an angel has been whispering to us? These things often appear to us to come from outside ourselves, as Socrates felt they came from his dæmon. We need not always believe that this is psychological projection. It could be that an angel is communicating with us.

Admittedly, there is no *need* of angels. Some Christians find they can get on quite well in their spiritual lives without believing in them. They are, spiritually, aware only of God and the human soul. That does not stop God from working with people in ways that they do not acknowledge, or from giving us more than is strictly necessary. He is a God of an unnecessary and incredible bounty. We do not *need* the prayers of the saints, or even the prayers of our friends. God can help us without them. That does not stop him from using them, and it does not stop us from appreciating them.

God could succour and defend us on earth without need of any angels; but in his amazingly prodigal generosity, he has created them and he allows some of them to come to our aid when we need their help. And he sometimes lets some of us catch a glimpse of them. For that, we can give him our grateful thanks.

I believe in God the Father Almighty, maker of heaven and earth, and of all things visible and invisible. If that is the kind of God in whom I believe, it would be incredible if the only living beings he had created were those on this earth. He is the Creator of the whole great Chain of Being which begins with his marvellous creatures in the heavens and ends with the rocks and stones of inanimate creation.

In the middle are we human beings, creatures of time who yet have eternity written into our hearts; made of physical matter but destined (if we will only open ourselves to God's promptings) to become creatures of unearthly glory.

Psychical and Spiritual

We are in the middle, between the angels and the beasts. We are not angels and we shall not become angels. The face of Stephen at his martyrdom may have been like the face of an angel (Acts 6.15), but the Psalmist knew that man had been created 'lower than the angels : to crown him with glory and worship' (Ps. 8.5 PBV).

Angels are another link in the Chain of Being, quite distinct from human beings. When Aunt Ada dies, it is incorrect to say that she has gone to be an angel. It would make as much sense to say she had gone to be a hippopotamus (actually, had you known the too, too solid flesh of *my* Great-Aunt Ada, you would realise that she was much more likely to end up as a hippopotamus than as an angel; but that is another matter).

So I believe in the existence of the angelic hierarchies.

The creation is more mysterious than we can ever imagine; and the veil between this world that we can see and the other world which we do not normally see, is a thin and shifting one - and sometimes, some people are allowed to have a glimpse of the things that are normally unseen, just to let the rest of us know that this world of God's making is not as plain and simple as we might think. That is one reason why there exists a Churches' Fellowship for Psychical and Spiritual Studies.

#

But, even if there are such beings as angels, are all of them good ones? Are there such entities as evil angels, devils, or demons? That is another question altogether.

If angels are God's messengers, it is certain that not all messages from God are either welcome or comforting. They may be, and for evildoers we are assured they are, often dire in the extreme. The 'message' which Ehud brought to the oppressive ruler Eglon ('I have a meesage for thee, O king') was delivered in eighteen inches of cold steel, as one can read in Judges 3.12-26. And if God's creatures are bringing God's message, even if it is a message of cold comfort, they are serving God and are to be thought of as good angels rather than evil ones. The Prayer Book Version of Psalm 78.50 may read that God 'cast upon them the furiousness of his wrath, anger, displeasure, and trouble : and sent evil angels among them', but the more accurate translation of the Revised English Bible speaks of God's 'blazing anger, ... wrath and enmity and rage' as his 'messengers of evil'. Perhaps that is why, in the apocalyptic paintings of Hieronymus Bosch and his like, the angels who are tormenting the wicked in hell are clearly enjoying themselves immensely. Why not? It is God's work they are doing.

But that is far from the whole story. Many things which happen in the world are a very long way away from being God's will. If the world created by God was 'very good', as we are assured in the first chapter of the book Genesis, how has this come to be? Is it all the fault of humankind for its self-seeking folly? Or is there something cosmic about evil, so that we should seek its origin in wills other than human? Certainly, evil seems to have existed in the world before mankind came upon it (unless we are to deny that animal suffering is anything to worry about), so we can hardly say that humanity is solely responsible for the twists of a crooked world.

Some of the Old Testament writers were so seized with the concept of God's omnipotence that they saw everything in the world, good and evil alike, as part of God's inscrutable handiwork. 'If disaster strikes a city, is it not the work of the LORD?', asked Amos (3:6), and the exilic prophet who wrote under the name of Isaiah (45.7) has God saying, 'I make the light, I create darkness; author alike of wellbeing and woe, I, the LORD, do all these things'. The writer of the book of Job wrestled long and hard with this question without reaching an intellectually, emotionally, or spiritually satisfactory answer.

The traditional Christian answer to the conundrum is that God created the angels, as he created us, with free-will, and that some of the angels, as we have done, misused that free-will and rebelled against their Creator. There is a hint of this doctrine in the New Testament. The second letter of Peter speaks (2.4) of 'the angels who sinned' whom God has consigned to the dark pits of hell, where they are held for judgement. But 2 Peter is hardly a central document of the New Testament, and unless its doctrines are reflected in more significant parts of Scripture, we must regard them as highly speculative.

Many people believe that, unlike the angels, who are created by God and are objective beings, evil entities are beings which we have ourselves created. They hover somewhere between the status of being real, self-existent, objective creatures in some kind of psychic dimension and being merely subjective creations of our own mental processes. Evil thoughts and plans and desires can coalesce together in such a way as to become temporary psychic entities in their own right, swirling around the spiritual atmosphere like an evil smoke, and ready to attack ill-advised or ill-intentioned folk. They can be strengthened if they are worked on. They wither away if they have no fresh psychic energy pumped in to them. They can be dispersed if a stronger and more spiritual power is directed against them.

It certainly seems to be the case that places which have been associated with evil or unhappiness can be affected for years, maybe even centuries, afterwards. These 'place memories' do not seem to retain any connection with the people who originally caused them. Sometimes they are only reactivated in a seemingly random way, and the event which caused them is repeated to the view of an onlooker. More often, the history of the place leaves a vague sense of unease which is picked up by psychically sensitive people who come to live there.

I have already briefly referred (on page 15 above) to some cases which have cropped up in my own experience; the student room where a previous occupant had indulged in dysfunctional sessions of magic, and the block of flats built on the site of the mortuary of a former parish workhouse. The first of these was put to rest by prayers and the application of holy water, and the second by a requiem Eucharist with special intention for the souls of the people whose mortal bodies had rested there. Less worrying place memories, like that occasional smell of warm wet coal to which I also referred, sensed in a house in an estate built over the remains of miners' cottages belonging to the days before pit-head baths, are best simply accepted as reminders of past history rather than thought of as suitable cases for treatment. And, to counter the depressing thought that it is only the evil that men do that lives after them, we should remind ourselves that holy places can have an almost palpable atmosphere built up over years of devotion, which exerts a genuine healing power over their visitors and pilgrims.

But, to return to the topic of evil entities, why should people want to create such revolting beings, or have anything to do with them, let alone to wish to welcome them and strengthen their powers? The two rival theologies in this respect are those of Augustine and Irenaeus. Augustine believed that mankind was corrupted through a primeval fall (the sin of Adam, the father of the whole human race) which twisted human nature and left it with a moral infection that has been passed on ever since, from generation to generation. Irenaeus believed that sin was more due to imperfection than to a fall from a primeval state of innocence, and that the human race has to learn to be more adult and less childish in its behaviour. But both believed that as we are now, we are subject, not only to our own human devices and desires, but to battles with non-human entities which constantly try to deflect us from doing what God would have us do.

We shall probably never reach agreement on whether it was God who created angels who sinned, or whether it is we who have endowed them with whatever degree of reality they possess. What is more certain than their origin is that the New Testament is firmly of the belief that these evil beings *do* exist, that they are of various levels of danger to us, and that there is one entity among them who is more dangerous than the rest of them put together.

Every writer in the New Testament mentions him. They usually give him the name Satan, though they sometimes use other names such as Beelzebul. Often they refer to him obliquely rather than naming him explicitly. Many Christians believe that the idea of a personal devil called Satan is simply a pre-scientific understanding of phenomena which psychology and medicine are better able to treat without any demonological hypotheses. Others (and I am among them) think that the New Testament may be more literally true than the 'liberals' are willing to concede.

The theological reasoning of these evil beings may be orthodox ('even the devils believe', says James 2.19, 'and tremble'), but their actions are firmly directed against anyone who tries to do the will of God. The work of Christians is not to understand how they came to be, but to resist them. 'Your enemy the devil', wrote St Peter (1 Peter 5.8-9), 'like a roaring lion, prowls around looking for someone to devour. *Stand up to him.*'

Not all wrongdoing needs to be blamed on Satan or his more junior demons. Some of it is no more than the result of unhappy miscalculation. That may be either moral miscalculation, in which case we call it folly, or mechanical miscalculation, in which case we say it is due to error. But often, wrongdoing is (in the words of the Confession in the *Common Worship* services) 'our own deliberate fault'. There is a temptation to do what we know is against the will of God, and we succumb to that temptation. The temptation may come from nothing more mysterious than our own desire, and, if so, there is no need to explain it as the work of any being or creature outside ourselves. But if the similar temptation is indulged in time and again, so that it hardens into a habit, the person who is tempted may begin to build up some kind of psychic entity which starts to have its own quasi-autonomous existence. Temptation unresisted is beginning to shade into obsession with an evil habit or practice, and resistance is becoming harder and harder - though not impossible, even without outside help. But obsession can easily shade into a further stage in which the evil is (or seems to be) objectively outside the person concerned, and yet taking them over, so that they no longer have the moral freedom even to wish to fight against it. We have moved from temptation, through obsession, to demonisation, and the victim needs outside help before they can be freed from the entity which has taken their life over.

This is an extreme case, and does not often happen. I am quite familiar in my own experience with the way in which temptations come to me again and again with distressing regularity, and I know I have to tell the entity that is behind them to get out of the way and stop bothering me. That is quite different from anything which needs an exorcism. (Incidentally, what most people describe as 'exorcism' is really the ministry of pastoral care; the pastoral care of those to whom the stresses and strains of relationships have caused poltergeist activity in their home or office or factory, the pastoral care of departed human beings whose post-mortem unhappinesses are causing continuing distress to those left behind on this earth, or the pastoral care of people who are worried by unsought psychic experiences.)

Exorcism should be necessary only on the very rarest of occasions, when a Christian is confronted by a person who is so in the grip of evil that they can neither escape from it by their own efforts, or even, in their worst moments, even *wish* to be rid of it. In the Anglican tradition a 'major exorcism' of this kind should only be performed by an authorised minister, and with the express permission of the diocesan bishop. It requires a great deal of preparation by the exorcising team, as well as long and careful pastoral care afterwards. Those Christians who claim to exorcise at the drop of a hat are often irresponsible publicity-seekers who can easily do more harm than good, and need to be avoided.

If the kind of demonisation calling for a major exorcism is a rare occurrence, there are, much more frequently, lesser psychic misadventures which do not require such drastic treatment. Troublesome entities, which can best be described as minor psychic powers wandering in some kind of spiritual back-water, can cause considerable trouble to people who unwisely or inadvertently disturb them. Some people are more psychically open than others, and may be able to receive telepathic impressions from living people or departed beings. Usually this causes no difficulty, but sometimes an openness to psychic impressions can lead to psychic invasion, and trouble lies ahead.

This is why people should not indulge in psychic experimentation without spiritual protection. 'Dabbling', or immature experimentation such as happens when teenagers try to get messages from a ouija board, is particularly hazardous. If there are such things as mendacious or ill-intentioned psychic entities which can work on human beings who allow them to take up residence, then opening one's psyche to any influence that might be around is as foolish as attempting a surgical operation without disinfectant. Even if there are no such things as evil spirits, then the ouija board is still dangerous. It can trigger deep and dormant psychological dysfunctions with disastrous effect. Playing with it is a way of bypassing the psychological censor which usually suppresses our subconscious desires for self-harm or for violence towards relatives or friends about whom our feelings are ambiguous. So, whether the ouija board is a method of contacting spirits or a way of accessing our subconscious mind, its use cannot be recommended.

Similarly, if anybody discovers that they have the kind of psychic or mediumistic sensitivity that enables them to contact discarnates, they should only exercise it in responsible ways, with prayer, and with guidance from a spiritually mature counsellor. Otherwise they may find too late that they have been in contact, not with the benign angels of God, but with malevolent entities set on destroying them. As St Paul warns us (2 Corinthians 11.14), it is easy to be misled, because even Satan can disguise himself as an angel of light.

To sum up: Christians may legitimately believe in the existence of superhuman beings sent by God from the realms of glory to help us in our earthly pilgrimage, but we need always to be on the lookout, because there is more than one kind of non-earthly entity, and not all of them are benign.

5

Post-mortem prospects

'Death', said Canon Scott Holland, 'is nothing at all. It does not count'. Or so said the straw man whom the Canon created in the sermon he preached in St Paul's Cathedral on the morning of Whit Sunday, in 1910.

The nation was in sombre mood. A couple of miles away, at Westminster, the coffin of King Edward VII lay in state awaiting his funeral, so Scott Holland preached about death. He began by outlining two different and irreconcilable ways of regarding it. The first would be to think of death as unmitigated disaster. It is 'blind and inexorable; ... it wrecks, it defeats, it shatters. ... It makes its horrible breach in our gladness with careless and inhuman disregard.'

'But', he went on, 'there is another aspect altogether which death can wear for us.' As we look at the face of a loved one who has died, it seems to say to us, 'Death is nothing at all. It does not count. I have only slipped away into the next room.'

Scott Holland went on to show how both those two ways of regarding death are natural, and how they both contain some truth; but how superficial both of them are when laid alongside the full Christian understanding. One is too brutal, the other is too sentimental.

It is a sad commentary on today's way of thinking that the description which begins 'Death is nothing at all' has been reprinted onto a million pieces of card, decked around with floral edging, and sent out to countless mourners as though it were Scott Holland's own belief and Christian orthodoxy. But then, as T.S.

Psychical and Spiritual

Eliot said, 'human kind cannot bear very much reality'.

Few of us think that the death of others does not count, and even fewer of us regard our own death in so cavalier a way. If, that is, we ever think about it at all. Earlier generations may have been exhorted to remember that mankind is inherently mortal, but the thought today is repressed into most people's sub-conscious and its disturbing implications are not allowed to come into the open. Yet nothing is more certain than that you will die. And so will I.

What, then, might be our post-mortem prospects?

The most obvious answer would be to say that, at death, we are extinguished. That answer is easy to envisage in relation to other people, but almost impossible for us to envisage for ourselves. Try it. You can imagine other people not existing, but you cannot easily imagine yourself simply ceasing to be. You can imagine your own funeral, or the attitude of other people when they hear of your death. You can imagine the distress of your relatives, or the pleasure of the charities whom you remembered in your will; but you are imagining *yourself* watching it, and if there is no longer any 'you', there cannot be any thing or person to do that watching. You might say, 'When I die, I shall know whether or not there is anything after death', but you will only be there to know if the answer is that there *is* something. If there is nothing after death, there will not be a 'you' to realise that 'you' have ceased to exist, so 'you' will never know that there is no such thing as post-mortem existence.

However, even if we believe that we will be extinguished when we die, we know that after our death, babies will continue to be born, and new centres of consciousness will come into being. At present (except on very rare occasions and in some rare states which are the province of parapsychologists) we are incapable of removing our consciousness from our physical bodies, let alone of inhabiting the body of any other being and experiencing their consciousness in the same way that we experience our own. But after our death, other consciousnesses will come into existence, each of whom will experience the world 'from inside' as we are now experiencing it 'from inside', and each of whom will be as self-encapsulated as we are now. The fact that *we* will by then have ceased to be conscious does not affect the fact that after our death, *someone* in the world will be as conscious, and will as consciously be living in the mess or paradise this generation has made of the world, as we are currently conscious. *We* will not be that person, and that person's life will not be in any way a continuation of our individual life. There will be no connection between that person and us. We, the people we now are, will not be experiencing their experiences. But conscious pleasure and pain and love and frustration and agony and ecstasy will exist after we have died. They will come to a person tortured in Burma or pampered in Hollywood; to a person healthy and fulfilled, or to a person dying in cancerous agony because they have lived their life under a depleted ozone layer. But that person will call themselves 'me', and will be every bit as aware of themselves as we are aware of ourselves now, and every bit at the centre of their own universe, and will find it every bit as impossible as we do, to inhabit anybody else's experience.

If it be the case that we do not survive death in any way, the very fact that human consciousness continues, and will continue after we are dead, should be a goad to us to do all we can to ensure that we pass on a better world for fresh consciousnesses to experience than we ourselves inherited.

The ultimate in believing that nothing of our person survives death is the stance of those who follow Dr Susan Blackmore. She believes that there is no conscious 'I' after death because there is none *before* death, either. To her, we are simply a concatenation of brain states which has achieved the amazing ability to be 'conscious' (whatever that is) of 'itself' (whatever *that* is). It is capable of learning through the action of 'memes', or elements of culture which are replicated and passed on from generation to generation by imitation. As soon as the brain structure disintegrates, that ability disintegrates with it. As Dr Blackmore says at the end of *The Meme Machine* (Oxford University Press, 1999),

> We can carry on our lives as most people do, under the illusion that there is a consistent conscious self inside who is in charge, who is responsible for my actions and who makes me me. Or we can live

as human beings, body, brain, and memes, living out our lives ... in the knowledge that that is all there is. Then ... we can be truly free - not because we can rebel against the tyranny ... but because we know that there is no one to rebel.

That is a bleak prospect, but it depends on an assumption. It only works if we assume that, because our awareness of being self-conscious whilst we are living in this world depends on the state of our brain cells, consciousness is nothing more than a by-product of brain activity. That is not a particularly modern point of view. The author of the *Wisdom of Solomon* in the Apocrypha wrote (2.2) that there were many people in his times who believed that 'our reason is a mere spark kept alive by the beating of our hearts'. But it is only an assumption. As any driver knows, his car will refuse to move if the sparking-plugs are defective. But for my car to go from my home to the supermarket, there has to be a driver as well as an efficient set of sparking plugs. So, *pace* Susan Blackmore, it is necessary to have a functioning brain to be alive in this world, but what is *necessary* may not be *sufficient*. It could just as well be that the brain with all its circuits and complications is the mechanism used by the personality to express itself in this world, just as the internal combustion engine with its sparking plugs is the mechanism used by the driver to get from A to B.

The question, however, still remains. Is this conscious 'I' of which I am aware, which uses brain activity to express itself in space and time, something which continues in any way after the dissolution of the brain which it is using here and now? Can the personality express itself in other spaces or other worlds or other dimensions by using different means, the nature of which will be beyond our comprehension until such time as we are living in one of those other worlds or spaces or dimensions? At any rate, there is nothing to prevent us from using that possibility as our working assumption and seeing where it takes us, just as Susan Blackmore has taken an opposite assumption and got where *she* is at present.

#

There are many possible scenarios. Reincarnation is one which is becoming increasingly popular today, but that single word hides a multitude of possibilities and problems. At its simplest and most popular, the idea holds that after I die, the essential part of me will carry on by inhabiting another physical body. It is the scenario we sketched out a page or two ago, except that the consciousness which comes into being at some future date *is* linked to my present consciousness.

That is not as trouble-free an assumption as it first seems. How can this consciousness be 'me' if it does not share my memories, my hopes, my emotions? What does it mean to say that 'I' am the 'same' person as someone who lived and died before I was born, when I cannot key in to his consciousness of himself? A person who undergoes complete amnesia is the same person as the one who suffered the trauma which wiped all memory out, because that person occupies the same physical body after it as beforehand. In the event of dying and being reincarnated, however, there is no such continuity to prove identity.

The great Eastern religions solve this conundrum in different ways, but in each case by denying that it *is* a conundrum. For Hindus, the individual soul or *atman* is indestructible, and is tied to the wheel of rebirth in a weary cycle of reincarnations, from which it can only escape by being identified with the supreme and ultimate transcendent reality or Brahman. The fact that we are not consciously aware of any of these former incarnations does not matter. What is objectively true is that the law of *karma* ensures that the life we are currently living is the moral result of the lifestyle of the *atman* in its previous incarnation. Buddhists, on the other hand, deny that there is any inherently existing *atman* or self to be the bearer of consciousness. The only reality is the consciousness itself which, in each of its particular incarnations, gives rise to a feeling of self. This feeling changes, constantly during each lifetime and profoundly between life-times, but it is an illusion, and the truly enlightened person can recognise it as such. So, once more, the fact that we do not remember past lives is no surprise.

Typical Westerners manage without either of these subtleties. This is because for them, individual identity and consciousness is of primary value, and they regard their own sense of self as supremely important. They do not want to die, and so they believe that 'they' will reincarnate once more, as they must have incarnated many times in the past. Some people believe that they and a group of their relatives or close friends have incarnated together many times over many centuries, so that the ties which bind them each to the other are of many lives' duration. Others are happy enough to expect to make new friends and be linked to new relatives in their new incarnation. This life may not have been wholly satisfactory for them, but, like students re-sitting an examination which they have previously failed, they hope that next time they may be able to do better. The fact that they will most probably, in their future incarnation, know nothing about this one, is of less importance than the fact that there will be a continuation of consciousness and experience. They do not necessarily believe that their present incarnation is the moral result of their previous one. They are more likely to believe that they have a voluntary choice of when and where to reincarnate, and whether to be male, female, rich, poor, intelligent, simple, or even whether to be human or animal. What is important to them is the possibility of adding further experiences, and wholly different *kinds* of experience, to the riches of the past, whilst working off its errors. Someone who has led the life of a rich Western male may believe that he needs the experience of being an oppressed woman living in third world squalor and poverty in order to become a fuller person.

The empirical evidence for reincarnation is partly psychological and partly parapsychological. It has been used to explain the existence of arithmetical geniuses who can tell you the square root of a seven-figure number within seconds, or of a musical genius such as Mozart, who had mastered the keyboard and was writing his own compositions at an age when most of us had not even started school. People like this must have retained their amazing talents from a previous life. Reincarnation has also been used as an explanation of the psychological phenomenon of *déjà vu*. When we go to a place we have never visited before, and it looks so familiar to us that we *know* what is round the next corner, might it not be that we have been there in some former existence, and our memory of it is being jogged in this way?

None of these arguments is water-tight. Childhood geniuses may simply be an example of the marvellous abilities of the human brain. They only amaze the rest of us because we, unlike them, are only using a tiny fraction of the brain's possibilities (never mind the brain; even the innards of my computer can do amazing things of which I am totally unaware because I am so technologically illiterate!). *Déjà vu* might be the result of our remembering a precognitive dream when we are awake and it is 'coming true'.

There is other evidence for reincarnation which is more parapsychological by nature. We have long known that skilled hypnotists can help their clients retrieve memories from many years back, and can help them to relive forgotten childhood traumas which have affected their psychological lives ever since. By an extension of this technique, some particularly skilled hypnotists can get their clients' memories to go even further back, and recall events which happened to them in former lifetimes. The classic example is the 'Bridey Murphy' case of the late 1950s, in which the hypnotist Morey Bernstein regressed a young American woman to nineteenth-century Ireland, so that she could give him a detailed account of her life and surroundings.

The difficulty with this method of recovering past-life memories is that hypnotism works because the client wishes to co-operate with the hypnotist. Sometimes, in order to do this with some degree of plausibility, the client will invent, quite subconsciously and without any overt wish to deceive, a complete fantasy world with fictional names and places. Basic archival or historical research will soon unmask such cases. Sometimes, the client will remember a historical novel they have read many years ago and will clothe their fantasy world with names and situations from it, besides accurately regurgitating its factual errors. If the parapsychological researcher is lucky enough, he may be able to discover this source material.

Sometimes, explanations like this are not so easy to accept. For an example, look at the case which Linda Tarazi recorded in 1990 in the *Journal* of the American Society for Psychical Research (Volume 84, pages 309-44). A middle-aged American woman, under hypnosis, told a colourful story of her former life. She claimed to have been a person named Antonia, who lived in Spain, North Africa and the West Indies in the sixteenth century. Antonia survived investigations by the Spanish Inquisition, had a hopeless love affair, and eventually drowned off the coast of a Caribbean island at the age of thirty-two.

Where did this story come from? The subject's own imagination, fuelled by a general historical education, in which case any competent historian would have been able to uncover anachronisms or errors? A book she had read years ago, in which case her memory was unlikely to be one hundred per cent accurate? Or from her own hypnotically recovered memories of when she was incarnate as Antonia? As Ms Tarazi writes, 'hundreds of hours of research over three years in two dozen libraries and universities, travel to Spain, North Africa, and the Caribbean, and correspondence with historians and archivists verified over a hundred facts, but uncovered no errors'. Regrettably, no evidence for the existence of Antonia herself could be found in any archive, but some of the statements she made in the course of her narrative could only be verified in sixteenth-century diocesan records in a remote Spanish city. Eventually, one of the statements made by the subject *was* tracked down in the library of the university which she had attended, and the suspicions of those who believed that this was the origin of her fantasy were immediately raised. But the book was in Spanish, over a hundred years old, and its pages had never been cut since its acquisition by the library. In any case, the subject neither spoke Spanish, nor could she read it.

The most prolonged and detailed investigation of reincarnation, however, is not along the lines of hypnotic regression. It is the monumental work of Dr Ian Stevenson of the University of Virginia and his collaborators, who have for the last thirty years or more been investigating cases of children who seem to have retained memories of previous lives. Dr Stevenson began this research with cases from India, but in the course of his work, cases have been investigated from places as far apart as Myanmar (Burma), Sri Lanka, Lebanon, Thailand, the United States, and Britain. These usually involve very young children aged between two and four, and their memories generally fade away by the time they are between five and eight years old. The children often, though by no means exclusively, come from cultures where reincarnation is an accepted doctrine. Usually they say that they do not belong to their present family, and they talk about the time they lived in another place. Their patterns of play may be consistent with the story they tell.

For an example of an English case (not one of Dr Stevenson's), we may cite the Pollock twins. Joanna and Jacqueline Pollock, sisters aged eleven and six, were killed in a road accident near their home in Hexham, in Northumberland. A year and a half later, their mother gave birth to identical girl twins. When they were four months old, the family moved thirty miles to Whitley Bay and did not revisit Hexham for another three years. But when they did, to their mother's astonishment, the twins knew where their sisters' old school, the playground, and the swings and slides were, and insisted that they knew the house where they had lived.

Dr Stevenson's earlier volumes were entitled 'Cases *suggestive of* reincarnation', but his researches have gradually allowed him to be more definite in accepting that that suggestion might be the true explanation of the phenomenon. Many of the cases involve children claiming to be the reincarnation of people who have died an early or a violent death, either in war, a violent affray, or as the result of an accident. The children in question may very likely have birth-marks, and these often correspond to the cause of death of the person whose reincarnation they purport to be. In the Pollock case, one of the twins had a thin white line on her forehead, similar to one which her dead sister got when she fell off her tricycle, and a pigmented mark on her left hip identical to one which Jacqueline had had.

As so often in parapsychology, the interpretation of all these data is far from straightforward. Perhaps they *do* prove the truth of reincarnation. But that is not a necessary inference. Even when we have eliminated the cases which are more easily explained by postulating the exercise of a vivid fantasy, or the client's suggestibility under hypnosis, there are many possible parapsychological explanations of the data. Our experience of 'place memories' inclines us to believe that there may be situations where psychic remnants of past lives may linger. They may not always be linked to particular places, but could be due to some degree of psychic affinity between the experiencers and the trace that they have picked up. People who believe they are reincarnations of former characters live their own lives most of the time. They only pick up occasional reminiscences or recognitions of places or people which link them to a supposed former lifetime. Psychically sensitive mediums regularly do as much, without believing that they are reincarnations of the departed people with whom they are in touch.

Sometimes, however, we come across cases where it is easier to believe in reincarnation than in any of the possible alternative scenarios. What do we make of them? The important thing to say is that what we believe of one, we do not have to believe of all. Each of us is an unique individual, and each of us has his or her own unique personality and needs. Perhaps that is why there is so much disagreement amongst reincarnationists as to when and in what form people are reincarnated. Some pundits say we are reincarnated almost immediately, others believe there may be centuries between reincarnations. Some say we must change sex at every fresh incarnation, others say it happens seldom. Some say we are reincarnated close to our old home, others say this is rare. Some say we may return as animals, others hold that this is no more than a metaphorical or symbolic statement. Some say that everyone will be reincarnated, others hold that a return to this earth is only necessary for those who have died a violent death or an unprepared one. Certainly the cases collected by Dr Stevenson contain more than their fair share of people who seem to have reincarnated after fatal accidents. *The Tibetan Book of the Dead* teaches that only those who approach their death with the correct thoughts and rituals are able to escape the wheel of rebirth. Christians in past ages used to teach the necessity of preparing for death in a responsible way. That particular devotional practice is not as prevalent nowadays, although even as late as 1980, when the Church of England was authorising the Alternative Service Book, it altered the wording of the Litany. The old Book of Common Prayer asked that we might be spared from 'battle, murder, and sudden death'. In the ASB, that was turned into a petition about the danger of 'dying unprepared'. Could it be that the danger of return is greater for those who are not ready for the life of whatever world there may be to come?

All this may indicate that even if reincarnation is possible, it is no Johnny-fit-all. But is it, in any form, a possible Christian doctrine? It is not a doctrine known to the Bible. True, there are a few texts which may be interpreted this way, but only by reading the doctrine into them rather than out of them.

For instance, there is the prophecy of Malachi (4.5) that God would send the prophet Elijah back to his people before the great and terrible day of the Lord. Some people believed that Jesus of Nazareth was a reincarnation of Elijah (Mark 8.28). Jesus himself appeared to pin the prophecy on to John the Baptist (he is reported in Mark 9.13 as saying, in connection with John, that 'Elijah has already come, and they have done to him what they wanted'), though the Fourth Gospel insists that John himself refused any such identification (John 1.21). But did the original prophecy of Malachi mean, literally, that he believed that the prophet Elijah was to be reincarnated? Or did it simply mean that he held that God would eventually send someone to Israel who would be as great as Elijah and would do the same sort of things as that great prophet of the past had done? It was certainly believed that when great prophets died, their spirit could rest on other people who carried on their work - people who were alive at that time, and who therefore could not in any sense be thought of as their reincarnations. So, when Elijah died, his spirit was said to have rested on his disciple Elisha (2 Kings 2.15), and when King Herod had John the Baptist executed, he feared that the same sort of thing had happened, and that John's spirit was motivating Jesus of Nazareth (Mark 6.14). It is most likely that Malachi was no more thinking of reincarnation when he spoke of God sending Elijah back to earth than Shylock was in *The Merchant of Venice*, when he called Portia 'a Daniel come to judgement'. According to the Gospel-writers, the prophecy was fulfilled when Elijah (the original Elijah, not a reincarnation of Elijah) *did* come back to earth and was seen by Jesus and his three close followers on the Mount of the Transfiguration (Mark 9.4), as a sign that the 'great and terrible day of the LORD' was about to arrive.

A more likely place where reincarnation may have been in the background is John 9.2. Jesus and his followers saw a man who had been blind from birth. They asked Jesus who it was who had sinned, the man or his parents, to deserve so great a punishment. The question presupposed that one possible answer would have been 'the man himself', in which case clearly he would have had to have sinned either in the womb or in a previous lifetime. (To sin in the womb was not thought a ridiculous notion. Fœtuses were considered capable of performing good or bad actions. The unborn John the Baptist leaped in his mother's womb when the mother of his future Lord paid her a visit.) But, when asked about the past of the man born blind, Jesus refused to answer the question. It was not a matter of sin, he said, but an opportunity for the works of God to be made manifest.

That incident shows that, during the ministry of Jesus, there was plenty of theological debate. Indeed, Josephus, a Jewish writer of later in the first century AD, tells us that some of the Pharisees were speculating about the possibility of reincarnation. But the controversy never got into the front line of debate, either in first-century Judaism or in subsequent centuries amongst the Christians. It was completely marginal. The earliest Christians were on fire with the news of the resurrection of Jesus and what that meant for their own prospects of resurrection. The thought of coming back reincarnated into this world rather than going on to a new and unimaginably splendid other world where they could join their heavenly Lord in glory, would have been considered a very second-rate option.

A good many of our contemporaries believe that reincarnation was a Christian doctrine until it was outlawed in the sixth century, but the evidence for such a point of view is as shaky as the evidence for the belief that it was taught in the Bible. The only serious Christian theologian to have toyed with the idea, and that as late as the third century AD, was Origen, and his ideas never caught on. He held, like the author of the apocryphal *Wisdom of Solomon* (8.19-20, quoted on page 23 above), that souls existed before they entered human bodies. How else, he asked, can we reconcile God's justice with the fact that humans are born so unequal both in soundness of body or in faculties of the soul? We must have existed before our births in some paradise where we could have acted either morally or wickedly, to justify the kind of earthly existence which the good God subsequently chose for us. Origen taught a doctrine of pre-existence in a heavenly realm, not of reincarnation to this earth. His teachings were formally declared anathema at the Council of Constantinople in 553. (Incidentally, there is no reason why God should not create new souls when and as required. The growing world population should be no embarrassment, either for doctrines of pre-existence or of reincarnation.)

However, the fact that reincarnation is neither biblical nor was it taught in Christian antiquity does not necessarily mean that it is wrong. Biblical faith itself has absorbed many ideas from non-Israelite cultures, and there is no reason why Christian theology should not do the same, so long as it does not compromise the basics of the historic creeds. What matters is that we can keep an open mind about the many different kinds of post-mortem prospect, because they may not be the same for all of us.

#

We still have not properly addressed the question of whether there are any post-mortem prospects at all. From what we have seen about the psychic faculty, it looks as if the human mind can act independently of the other dimensions of this material world, so it is not as crazy as it might sound to believe that a mind could continue in existence after the body associated with it has disintegrated. But is there any empirical evidence that my human consciousness will continue in any way after the death of my physical body?

There is plenty, and of many kinds.

For instance, many a bereaved person has felt the presence of their loved one with them after his or her death. Some have even been able to be aware of their presence by the evidence of their senses. Dr Dewi Rees, writing in the *Christian Parapsychologist* for September 2000 about a survey he carried out when he was a GP in mid-Wales, tells us that his research

> showed that about 50% of widowed people have some experience of the dead spouse. Usually this is 'a sense of the presence' (39%), but some see (14%), hear (12%), or feel touched by (3%) their dead spouse. These perceptions are not restricted to the widowed. I have recently received letters from a brother and sister - writing separately - telling me that they sometimes detect their mother's presence by a distinctive smell in the house. They live in different localities but they both describe the same smell - a mixture of their mother's favourite perfume (Yardley's Freesia) and of the slight incontinence she acquired with increasing age.

'Crisis apparitions' are another, and a more dramatic, class of evidence. They seem to be less often reported nowadays than they were in former times, when communication over long distances was less immediate than it is today, but they are still reported. I have already mentioned (on page 14 above) the occasion when I was told by a Jesuit father about the time he went on retreat and saw a colleague of his on the terrace reading his breviary, and discovered later that his friend had never got to the retreat house because he had been involved in a fatal accident on his way there. Stories like that, which can be multiplied a thousandfold, can certainly lead us to believe that what has been seen is the immaterial ghost of the person who has survived death and returned to tell his friend about it.

This sort of thing does not only happen at the time of the death of the person whose apparition is seen, though crisis apparitions may strike us as more dramatic. For instance, the *Christian Parapsychologist* for March 2001 contains the following account of what once happened to an acquaintance of Professor David Fontana. The person concerned was a professional woman in her fifties who had had only one other psychic experience in her life.

She said,

> I was on a residential yoga retreat and one day, during a walk through the woods, Brian, one of the founder members of our group who had recently died, was suddenly standing next to me. He stood as tall as in life, a big smile on his face, but not quite solid. I would describe him as semi-transparent. He placed his hand on my shoulder and we walked together through the woods. I was struck by his left hand which had two deformed fingers - a birth defect - and I said to him, 'Oh, Brian, I thought we were mended when we get to heaven'. Brian walked beside me for about a minute and then he disappeared just before we left the wood.

There are also cases, well known to those who work in the deliverance ministry, where places retain for years, sometimes for centuries, memories of things that happened there, and the people to whom they happened. I have already discussed some examples of this in chapter 4 above. Often, the deliverance team will be called in to help where it looks as if a departed soul is tied to a place and is unable to move on its post-mortem journey, or where there has been unfinished business of some sort or other. There may have been a relationship which has been fractured and needs to be mended or a wrong that needs to be set right. Such accounts are the raw material of folk lore. St Augustine in the fifth century AD told the story of a widow who was being sued to repay money which the creditor claimed was owed him by the woman's husband. A vision of her dead husband revealed to her the whereabouts of the IOU which proved the creditor to be a fraud.

Other evidence for survival of death comes from the way in which some people who are dying, or who have narrowly escaped death, have been able to tell us how they glimpsed something of the other side of the great divide. The classic study of death-bed visions was published by Sir William Barrett as long ago as 1926, but in more recent times two parapsychologists, Erlendur Haraldsson and the late Karlis Osis, carried out field research with doctors and nurses in America and India who were able to tell them about their observations of hundreds of dying people. Many of them as they were dying had visions of loved ones or religious figures who were there to help them over their great transition. There were minor cultural differences between the experiences of the American and the Indian patients, but Osis and Haraldsson were able to show that in neither case were they drug-induced or psychotic. There have been cases (Barrett's study includes several) where the dying person saw helpers waiting whom their surviving relatives knew had died, but the news of whose death had been withheld from them.

And then there is the near-death experience. We have already mentioned stories of people who have been left for dead but who have recovered to tell others of their experiences. Some patients who survived a major accident or a heart attack have come back with accounts of having travelled into a horrifying pit, where blackness and despair have surrounded them and they have become convinced that their past life-style has been unacceptable, so that when they are resuscitated they resolve to live a better life. This kind of 'hellish' experience seems to be less frequent than the one where the patients have seen their own inert bodies at the scene of the accident or on the operating table, and have then passed through a dark constricting space into a place of brilliant light, where the colours are brighter than anything they have ever experienced in this world. They may review the salient events of their past lives and see what praise or blame attaches to them; then they meet deceased friends or relatives, or a 'figure of light', but are told their time has not yet come and they must, however unwillingly, go back to earth.

As with death-bed visions, there are minor cultural differences in near-death experiences related in different parts of the world, and most experiences only go part of the way along the above scenario, but the core facts of reports from various parts of the world seem to indicate that the experience is basically human rather than an artefact of prior religious or cultural belief. Today, there is an International Association for Near-Death Studies, which provides counselling and support for people who have undergone near-death experiences, and which publishes its scholarly *Journal of Near-Death Studies* to investigate the phenomenon and to try to find ways of understanding it.

Finally, there is the evidence which comes from psychic sensitives. Mediums claim to be able to communicate with entities in other dimensions, and to bring back messages from those we have loved, but lost because of death. The publications which the Society for Psychical Research has issued over the last hundred and twenty years, let alone the contents of the Society's library, contain more evidence, and more informed critical discussion of the evidence, than is possible for one person to master.

Much of it is a sad tale of human fallibility. There is plenty of evidence of fraud, and of guesswork based on the reading of subtle clues inadvertently given to mediums by sitters. But when the chaff has been blown away, we are left with some pure wheat. It looks as if some mediums are sometimes able to tell their clients things about their dead friends that only the departed friends could have known, and the truth of which has only been able to be established through careful archival or family research.

The SPR's *Journal* for January 2001 contains the record of a very careful American study in which a number of professional mediums were invited, one after the other, to give a sitting for a client who was placed behind a screen so that visual cues were impossible, and who was only allowed to answer 'yes' or 'no' to their questions or statements. Careful statistical analysis showed that the mediums had an almost uncanny ability to speak about the client's departed relatives and pets as if they could see them and find out things about them. A 'control' group of non-mediums was told only that the client was an Arizonan woman aged forty-six who had had multiple bereavements during the last ten years. They were asked to guess the answers to seventy questions about her. Their guesses were pathetically off the mark, whereas the mediums' statements contained correct answers in 77% to 93% of cases.

One or two parapsychologists have tried to set up experiments whereby they undertake to pass on a 'secret message' via a psychic sensitive after their death. Dr Robert Thouless in the 1940s wrote a sentence in what he believed to be unbreakable cipher, so that if he were able to communicate a two-word phrase after his death, it would enable the message to be decoded. Sadly, he did it all before modern computers had been developed, and some years after his death a laptop in America showed that the phrase 'Black Beauty' made perfect sense of the mishmash of letters in the code message.

My friend the Reverend Dr Charles Fryer has for many years been practising 'automatic writing'. He holds a writing implement in his hand and lets it move over the paper of its own volition. Instead of meaningless squiggles, what is left on the paper purports to be a series of messages from his father, who died many years ago. Charles writes his own questions or comments on the paper, and the automatic writing then responds appropriately. He is far from uncritical, and is aware that he could be self-deluded, but he wishes to make one further experiment to test whether survival is a possibility. He cannot complete it until after his death. He has left a tape with me which holds the text of a poem he has composed but which he has never written down, and which he has only spoken once. He intends to remind himself of it daily whilst he remains alive and to attempt to communicate it after his death. He has published the opening line so that after his death, it may be spoken to psychic sensitives to help jog what might be his foggy post-mortem memory. A number of sensitives have tried to complete the poem before his death, but without success. If they can do so after his demise, it will indicate that he has been able to make contact by this means.

#

All this material is highly suggestive. But can it *prove* anything? There is more than one way of interpreting the evidence, and the interpretation we put on it seems to depend greatly on what we believe about the inherent likelihood of human survival of death.

Thus, for example. A person who has actually had an experience of seeing a loved spouse some time after their death, may realise in it the continuing presence of their loved one, but those who have not may well brush it off as a 'bereavement hallucination'. Just as those who have lost a limb but retain the nerves and muscles which led to it can be fooled into believing that it is still present, so the person who has been close to a spouse throughout a long married life can be so used to seeing them sitting in their accustomed chair that they continue to do so when they are momentarily forgetful.

A survivalist interpretation of the crisis apparition is not the only possible one. My Jesuit friend could have been telepathically aware that something dire was happening to his colleague, and his unconscious could then have dressed this awareness up in the guise of a hallucination of the colleague doing the sort of thing that he would be expected to be doing, instead of the thing that was actually happening to him. Or the whole thing could be a mixture of an over-active imagination and a fortuitous coincidence.

As for non-crisis apparitions like the one of Brian in the woods, we do not even need the hypothesis of fortuitous coincidence to explain them. Over-active imagination can do it all. The same can be said for place memories. And incidents ostensibly involving the unquiet dead also involve the unquiet living, who want unfinished business to be over and done with, or need to know the whereabouts of IOUs they mislaid on an earlier occasion.

Death-bed visions and near-death experiences have spawned a whole multitude of psychological or neuro-physiological explanations, ranging from the power of folk-religion to trigger hallucinations in the dying, to the most sophisticated scenarios detailing what particular chemicals in the cells of what particular part of the brain would be likely to cause what particular experiences in a patient whose mental and physical processes were close to collapse.

And, finally, the evidence of mediumship is equivocal. Guesswork on the part of the medium can be a very fruitful source of relevant information, particularly when she observes how the sitter reacts to suggestions she makes to him. But even if all possibilities like that are excluded by careful design of the séance, any correct information about a departed person which comes via a psychic sensitive is either known to the sitter at the time, in which case the simplest explanation for it is that the medium has tapped into the sitter's memories and dressed them up as though they were messages from the departed communicator; or they are discovered through later research. In that case, who is to say that the medium was not clairvoyantly aware of the contents of the documents containing that information, or pre-cognitively able to access the sitter's mind at the time in the future when he verified the medium's statement?

Arguments like this are not the end of the story, by a long chalk. Experiments have been devised to make these non-survivalist explanations difficult or impossible. Sceptics have countered with increasingly sophisticated counter-arguments; and so it goes on. People who are convinced of the possibility of survival point to the number and variety of kinds of evidence which have been adduced in its favour. Each individual strand of evidence has its weak points, but add them all together, and we can see that they all point in the same direction. Together, they make a stronger case than they could ever do if each part of the evidence was on its own. You can snap a single stick, but a bundle of ten is much harder to break. To which the sceptic's answer is that ten leaky buckets hold no more water than one; and so the argument goes to and fro.

In fact, we are back again with the situation we outlined in our first chapter, when we were thinking of the way in which scientific theories are modified, and the way, for instance, in which the Ptolemaic theory of the heavens was superseded by the Copernican. Our reading of evidence will depend on our overall paradigm of what sort of a world we imagine it is in which we are living.

If we are convinced that it is a world where anything except human survival of bodily death is, in principle, allowable, then we will be glad of any arguments which show us that the evidence is flawed and a non-survivalist explanation of the data is possible. If we believe we are living in a world where we can think of mind as being independent of body (though usually requiring body for its manifestation) then we will not imagine the survival of mind without body as inconceivable. And if we believe we live in a world which has a divine Creator behind it, and who is known in a man called Jesus of Nazareth who rose from the dead and gave proof of his continuing life to his followers, then we will be predisposed to regard the kinds of evidence that have been outlined in the last few pages as worth considering.

Worth considering, but not the sort of evidence that will convince the determined sceptic. In other words, if we believe in human survival of death, we are relying on faith rather than proof. It is not an unreasonable faith. We have reasons for believing. Some of those reasons are to do with the existence and nature of God, some are to do with the reliability of the New Testament documents, some are to do with empirical facts which are investigated by parapsychologists. For some of us, all these facts point in the same direction, and we are satisfied that life on this earth is not all there is. But God does not want us to be *forced* to believe in him. He will give us hints that help to strengthen our beliefs, but he seems to want human beings to trust him rather than demand cast-iron assurances from him. He will not be put to the test; he is sovereign and will not be put in the dock by human inquisitors.

#

If there *is* conscious life in store for us after our physical death, what kind of life is it, and where and how can it be experienced?

As we have already seen, reincarnation is one possibility, though if it is not accompanied by at least some memory of the previous life, it is hard to put an empirical meaning to it. I *may* have some connection with a person who lived and died before I was born, and this *may* affect my life-style or even my instinctive habits; but if I know nothing about it, it is a piece of useless information.

Or perhaps reincarnation is only the fate of a few? Not every child (by a long chalk) remembers a previous existence or shows birthmarks or play-patterns which are reminiscent of someone belonging to a previous generation. Perhaps only some of us come back. One of the insights about humanity which has become more and more clear to us in recent centuries is the individuality of every human being. My DNA is unique to myself, and my fingerprints are shared by no-one else. Nor are my soul-prints. We do not have to believe that every human being has identical post-mortem prospects. The evidence from parapsychology and elsewhere may favour a reincarnationist hypothesis in some cases, but that does not mean it must be true in every case.

According to St John (3.15, 8.51, 10.28, 11.26), Jesus only promised eternal life to those who found God through him, and we need to take these words seriously. We can believe in the resurrection of the body and the life of the world to come without necessarily believing the same as our forebears did about the route to that resurrection and that life, and without believing that every human being comes to it by the same route.

Perhaps those whose spiritual paths have not yet encountered the truth as it is in Jesus are tied to the wheel of repeated incarnations until they *have* met him and responded positively to his offer of life eternal. That might explain why cases suggestive of reincarnation are more frequent in non-Christian cultures. It is perhaps noteworthy that cases of children who claim to remember a previous life are rare in South India, where one in five of the population is Christian, whereas in North India, with a far smaller Christian population, cases are very numerous indeed.

We must, however, never forget 'that God has no favourites, but that in every nation those who are god-fearing and do what is right are acceptable to him' (Acts 10.34). The One in whom we find eternal life is not necessarily the explicit Christ of our own faith. He may be savingly implicit in places where he is not explicitly named, but where love, justice, and the knowledge of the unseen world fuel the actions of religious people.

If we want a *guaranteed* promise of eternal life, we shall certainly never be able to reach it through parapsychological data alone. They cannot provide that assurance. To begin with, not everyone who has died seems to be able to make contact with us through psychic sensitives. That may mean that they do not want to do so, or that they do not need to do so, or that they are not able to do so; but it could be interpreted as meaning that only a very few of us (i.e. the few who can communicate) survive.

It is also obvious that communications through sensitives do not last for ever. This could be because, once communication has been established, enough has been said to satisfy our need for assurance, and the communicators can then get on with their new life without worrying any longer about those they have left behind. Or it could mean that they have passed beyond the immediate post-mortem world to an existence from which it is not possible to communicate with earth. Or it could indicate that they only survive for a while and then fade away.

Again, phenomena such as place memories might indicate that what survives and communicates is only a fragment of a personality, a psychic shell, or a mere disintegrated component of humanity, condemned like Sisyphus to repeat for ever a set of semi-automatic and pointless random performances.

Not everybody who comes close to death and is resuscitated, has a near-death experience. This might be because not everybody survives to experience anything after their death. Even if every person who had a close touch with death *did* come back with accounts of their experiences, the most we could say would be that these people had had experiences for a brief time after their physical bodies had ceased to function. After that, do they go on to further experiences, which may be more demanding and less pleasant? Or do they peter out and end in oblivion?

So we can go on and on, asking interminable and unanswerable questions about how to interpret the ambiguous data of parapsychology. This is not to say that parapsychological data only hold out cold comfort. What they *do* indicate is that if we want to be able to assert anything about our post-mortem prospects, we need to go beyond the parapsychological data into realms of philosophical or theological speculation.

That may need some lateral thinking. For instance, are we sure we are self-encapsulated individual beings? In this life, we are not able to have windows into other people's souls (except in the fleeting moments when telepathy is operating), but perhaps each of us as an individual is only part of what we might call a 'group soul', like a peeled orange with a dozen or more segments. Every now and again, one segment will incarnate on planet earth, live its life, have its experiences, grow and mature, and then return to enrich the complete orange. Dr Kenneth Ring has speculated that the 'Being of Light' which some people see in their near-death experiences may be this total self with which we are united at the point of death. That kind of speculation ought not to be entirely strange to Christians who believe that, many as they are, they are part of a single Body of Christ in a Kingdom of Heaven in which relationships are as important as any kind of individual satisfaction.

Others believe that death is a fragmentation rather than a reunion. Peter Novak, in *The Division of Consciousness* (1997), explores the idea that what happens at death is that the human soul and spirit divide and go their separate ways. The spirit is the conscious mind and the soul the unconscious. When the conscious is no longer undergirded by the unconscious, it loses its memory, so that the spirit wanders earthbound without memory or individuality until it can reincarnate. When it *does* reincarnate, it has no recollection of its former existence, except in rare cases. On the other hand, the unconscious when not in contact with the conscious can have no further input, but is trapped in its own memories and fantasies. If its incarnate life has been well-integrated, this can be a heavenly existence. If not, life for what survives is a hell in which (to quote what the hymn-writer Isaac Watts wrote in 1709) 'thoughts, like old vultures, prey upon their heart-strings'. So both possible post-mortem scenarios are true. One part of us is reincarnated; the other goes to heaven or hell according to our earthly deserts.

That is an intriguing and novel speculation, but one which it would be hard to square with the kind of belief in the indivisibility of the human person which we developed in chapter 2 above, and which we saw to be characteristic, not only of St Paul, but also of much modern thinking.

These are not the only possible ways of interpreting the data of parapsychology. We need a larger canvas on which to paint the picture of our post-mortem prospects, and, for Christians, this will be one in which the loving care of almighty God is directed towards each human soul, so that what happens to each individual is for his or her greater and most lasting good. It is hard to believe that extinction or fragmentation would be consistent with the love of God and his promise that he will never, ultimately, forsake us. Nor will a lonely eternity in which we continue as individual selves without interacting with other human beings, especially those who have been significant to us during our earthly life. The Christian faith is an inescapably community affair.

The Christian hope is that we shall escape from the futility of an unending human immortality (which might turn out to be very bad and boring news) into the Gospel life of Resurrection. The typical mediumistic description of the life of the world to come seems more like Hades than paradise. But we have to admit that our human imaginative powers may not be bold enough to envisage precisely what he has in store for us. 'Eye hath not seen, nor ear heard, neither have entered into the heart of man, the things which God hath prepared for them that love him' (1 Corinthians 2.9, KJV). We will have to trust God and wait and see.

#

This means that death is real, and death is significant. The straw man whom Canon Scott Holland knocked down in the sermon with which we began this chapter, is wrong. Death is *not* nothing at all. It *does* count. When we die, we will do more than simply slip unchanged into the next room. Socrates, the philosopher, could face his own death with equanimity, and discuss the immortality of the soul over a glass of hemlock with his friend Crito. Jesus of Nazareth was not a philosopher who had a rational belief in the immortality of the human soul. He was a prophet who believed he was in the front line of the battle between the forces of his Father and the forces of irrationality and chaos. He did not face his own death with an attitude of calm detachment. He went to the Garden of Gethsemane and prayed in agony that the cup he had to drink might be taken from him; and his sweat was like great drops of blood falling on the ground. What he feared was not the natural horrors that lay ahead, but the supernatural terrors of a journey into completely uncharted territory.

When I contemplate my own death, I prefer to be comforted, not by the calm rationality of Socrates, but by the prospect of the companionship of someone who faced up to all its terrors and came through on the other side. I do not know what will happen to me after I die. I do not always feel that I know whether, after my death, there will be any 'me' which can have any experiences at all. A lifetime's study of the ambiguous evidence of parapsychology has left me less certain than I was when I started. There are times when the whole idea of its being possible for there to be conscious experience after the death of the body seems preposterously unlikely. And yet I cannot be satisfied with the feeling that the whole scenario is absolutely impossible. I find myself, repeatedly, being drawn back to the resurrection of Jesus and into the insights into the mind of God which he opened up for us. To accept that Jesus was resurrected, and to accept the consequences of that resurrection for our own post-mortem prospects, is a matter of faith. But it is a faith which comes and hits me with fresh power after every bout of agnosticism. If God be God, and if his love for us be anything like Jesus showed us, could he desert us when our flesh and bones have worn out? Could he who has designed us to be transformed into his very nature, snuff us out like a spent candle?

John Donne, Dean of St Paul's in the seventeenth century, had attacks of the same doubts, so he is a good guide for us when we are in the same position. When he was dangerously ill and thought he was near death, he wrote his *Hymn to God, my God, in my sickness.* He goes through his various sins, and asks God to forgive them - with a repeated pun on his name John Donne. He says, again and again, when he has confessed some of his sins,

Post-mortem prospects

'when thou hast done, thou hast not Donne, for I have more'. But then he comes to the last verse:

> I have a sin of fear, that when I've spun
>   My last thread, I shall perish on the shore;
> But swear by thyself, that at my death thy Son
>   Shall shine, as he shines now and heretofore;
> And, having done that, thou hast Donne:
>   I fear no more.

6

Christian parapsychology

It will be obvious to those who have read thus far that I believe the human psychic faculty is important, especially to those in whom it is well-developed. It is part of the way in which God has created the world and developed the human race, and therefore Christians ought to be ready to accept it and use it to God's glory.

Some people find the whole area of the psychic threatening and frightening. They don't understand it and they have a vague kind of unformed fear that if they get embroiled within it, all sorts of nasty things will begin to happen to them - their minds might get taken over and they could be dragged into a situation where they are powerless to resist forces about which they don't actually know anything, except that they can't do them any good. There are Christians who are like that, and often they lash out against everything remotely connected with the psychic faculty, because they are afraid of it.

There used to be a Christian periodical published in Hong Kong and dedicated to the cause of inter-religious understanding. It was called *Areopagus*, and its Editorial for Easter 1993 was on this very subject. If Christians are afraid of the psychic, the editor wrote, it is serious:

> We suspect something is evil, but we don't know why. This undifferentiated fear points to a much deeper problem : a suspicion that God just might not be able to help us if we get into trouble. ... [But] we worship a God who entered into an evil world and defeated the demons of fear for all time. If the world is going to hear the message of Jesus Christ over the din of religious pluralism, that message must be proclaimed by believers who are prepared to face

the unknown, to face the challenges of other faiths, to face their own fears.

It is, of course, true that unwise use of the psychic faculty can be dangerous. The same is true of unwise use of many of the faculties with which God has endowed us. Some people cannot control their appetite for sex, or alcohol, or money. But there is nothing to be afraid of in the exploration of any human faculty, provided it is entered with prayer and a sense of utter dependence on a God who loves the human race and is strong enough to protect any human being who trusts him.

Two attitudes in particular can help to banish that fear of the psychic from those who suffer from it. One is knowledge, and I hope that this book will have helped dispel the fear born of ignorance; but the greater is that perfect love which casts out fear (1 John 4.18). If we know that we are protected by the love of our Creator, there is no need to be afraid.

For most of its history, however, the Church has done little to dispel the fear which stems from ignorance about things psychic. People who claimed psychic insights were felt to be 'difficult', and their insights were suppressed, despite the ubiquitous place of the psychic dimension in the pages of the Bible. The main reason for this was regrettable, but true. The leaders of any religious group tend to have their own answers to their theological questions and to distrust anybody who might suggest to the faithful that it could be legitimate to have any alternative way of looking at things. That can lead to persecution of any deviant belief whenever the dominant religion has got sufficient of an upper hand. As Jeremy Taylor wrote in the Preface to his *Holy Living* (in 1650), 'when religion puts on armour, it may have the power of the sword, but not the power of godliness'. Religion in power is uniquely dangerous. The Taleban is an obvious recent example.

The Israelite priests and prophets in Old Testament times realised that the Canaanite religion was perilously attractive to the majority of their people, and the religious leaders of the Jahwistic cult had to make sure that in Jahweh's state, Canaanite

Psychical and Spiritual

practices were outlawed. So when Saul was powerful enough, he banished all the psychics from the land (1 Samuel 28.3), as Josiah did in his own reforms a few centuries later (2 Kings 23.24). In the New Testament, we come across Christian prophets and psychics (like Agabus in Acts 11.28 and 21.10), but if anyone tried to exercise such powers outside the Christian community, they got short shrift indeed. We have already (page 55 above) come across the cautionary tale of what happened to the seven sons of Sceva, who wanted to perform exorcisms 'in the name of the Jesus whom Paul preached' (Acts 19.14). They were not genuine followers of Paul or Jesus, so the person whom they were trying to exorcise flew at them, exclaiming, 'Jesus I recognise, Paul I know, but who are you?' and handled them with such violence that they ran out of the house battered and naked.

The idea was put about by the ecclesiastical leaders that there were certain facts which mankind was not *meant* to know, and about which it would be impious to enquire. Knowledge about things to do with the earth might be vouchsafed to humankind, but knowledge about realms beyond it was the preserve of God (Psalm 115.16). If God so decided, he could grant knowledge of this kind by special revelation, but that was his prerogative. Proud humans might try to unlock the divine secrets, but if they did, they would be in for trouble.

That is not an entirely unworthy or anti-intellectualist attitude. Some kinds of knowledge are harmful to us, and they can easily be used by evil men to disastrous effect. Should we be researching, for example, into germ warfare? Or should we be using human embryos as experimental material? Or carrying out the sort of medical procedures that were done in some of the more notorious Nazi establishments in the nineteen-forties? The answers are not as clear-cut as some people make out. Right ends do not make wrong means legitimate, and there are certain kinds of medical and psychological manipulation which it would be unethical to carry out on human material. But the fact that knowledge might be misused is no argument for forbidding the search for it. Scientific advance will be carried forward, and we shall have to learn to live responsibly with the knowledge that we gain. It will not always be easy. There are moral dilemmas and practical risks a-plenty in the application of our present scientific knowledge, and there will be many more (and more difficult ones) as this twenty-first century runs its course. We will have to learn how to live with knowledge, for example, about human genetics and about genetic manipulation both of plants and of sentient beings. We cannot simply say that research into those areas must cease in case we are unable to control the new knowledge that will come to us. Pandora's box cannot be closed, ever, again. Scientific progress is exciting, and although it is also dangerous, the dangers cannot stop it advancing.

What goes for scientific research in general, goes also for research into parapsychology. There are people who oppose it on the grounds that it aims to replace faith with knowledge. We know enough already, they say, by divine revelation, to be able to live our lives in the way God has mapped out for us. Any more knowledge would serve simply to feed human curiosity and human pride. If we magnify human discovery above divine revelation, we will begin to trust in ourselves rather than in God. We shall be inclined, for example, to believe that human immortality is a fact of natural science, and nothing to do with our relationship with God.

That kind of attitude will not wash in parapsychology, any more than it does in other branches of science. Truth will out, and when it is out, it is up to us as moral beings to make use of it in ways which glorify God rather than in those which glorify human pride. Parapsychological discoveries may throw light on human destiny beyond the grave, and if they do, it will be because God has enabled us to search the matter out, as he enabled other scientists in earlier centuries to discover the circulation of the blood or the map of the human genome. It will be for us as Christians to square that new knowledge with our traditional faith. Christians in Galileo's time had to square their theology with the new discoveries about the solar system. Christians in the nineteenth century had to take on board the Darwinian chronology without destroying their faith that the Bible contained God's Word for humanity. In our case as well as theirs, there will be turmoil as new insights are grafted onto an ancient system of truth, and how it will be done we cannot know in advance; but if we believe that God is truth and God is one, then theological truth can never be gained at the expense of denying scientific and parapsychological truth.

It may be that we *shall* discover as a scientific fact that humanity is destined for life after physical death. If so, that may become for theologians as much a primary datum as is the fact that human beings reproduce by sexual intercourse. It will still remain that if that is the way God has, in fact, made the world, it is up to us to find a satisfactory answer to the question 'why?'. That will be an inescapable theological question, though it will be asked as a result of there being scientific data behind it, and the answer will be found, not in the scientific data, but in what we can know of the nature of God and his relationships with the human race.

In fact, as we have seen, the discoveries of parapsychology in the matter of human destiny have in them more of inference than of proof, and it seems as though this will remain so in perpetuity. But it would be rash to assume so. Perhaps the twenty-first century will bring even this avenue of human study into the realm of proven fact.

But not yet. For the present we must take psychic sensitivity as a puzzling area of human ability, which holds out tantalising promises, but is still more a matter of faith than of certainty.

#

That being so, what ought to be the attitude of the Christian church to it, and how should Christians who believe they have some degree of psychic sensitivity live their psychic lives in a spiritual way?

In previous centuries, the Christian authorities were not very kind to such people. When they were in power, the ecclesiastics cracked down upon the folk healers and the psychics who claimed powers which were not under their sole jurisdiction.

They called them 'witches', whether the term was accurate or not (mediumship and witchcraft are quite different things, but the woman with psychic gifts about whom we read in 1 Samuel 28 was called the 'Witch of En-Dor' in the chapter heading of the King James Bible, and the title has stuck ever since). They invented all sorts of fictions about psychic sensitives which were supposed to make all decent Christians shun their ministrations, and when they could, they used inquisitions and witch-hunts to stamp them out. They side-lined their visionaries like William Blake and Emanuel Swedenborg, and (because by then the Church was no longer politically capable of direct persecution) it treated such Johnny-come-lately religions like Spiritualism with haughty disdain. The religious establishment does not like any source of power or any source of influence, let alone any authority, other than its own, and it will do its utmost to make sure that the faithful have only one set of leaders.

We can freely admit that the religious establishment has usually been heavy-handed in the way it has treated the psychic dimension. This should not lead us to make the equal and opposite error, and to say that all the claims made by people with psychic gifts, or all the religious or metaphysical ideas they come up with, are true and ought to be accepted. Often, they most definitely ought not. People with psychic sensitivity believe that what they know about the psychic realm, they know from direct and first-hand experience. That, naturally, is primary. The secondary tendency then is for them to begin to build up their own system of religious belief on the basis of their psychic experiences, untrammelled by any of the constraints of theological correctitude, thus offending orthodox religious believers. But Christians should neither reject the religious beliefs of all psychic sensitives out of hand nor swallow them wholesale, but treat them seriously and assess them critically. Neither persecution nor ridicule are adequate reactions.

When the psychic faculty becomes the basis of the whole of a religious system, a serious and critical examination shows it to be wanting in a number of ways.

Psychical and Spiritual

That is because psychic sensitivity is not the most important human faculty. Even in those people who possess it to an extraordinary degree, and are able to know when it is being exercised and in some degree to control it, it is usually fleeting and evanescent. It is never possible to be one hundred per cent sure that it is being exercised, and even less to be sure that its insights in any particular instance are genuine. Every psychic 'hunch' needs to be critically tested, and can only be accepted after careful examination.

There is another, even more important, reason why the psychic faculty cannot be made the centre of a complete religious system. Our human lives and loves matter supremely to us, and we want to know whether it is really true that 'love is stronger than death'. We develop into ourselves as unique personalities by our interactions with the people with whom we share our lives and to whom we give our love and loyalty, and when death severs those interactions, we lose a valuable part of our own selves. Similarly, the sense of being 'me' is at the centre of any human consciousness, and therefore the destiny of that 'me' is important. But if human lives and loves, and their continuance after death, are regarded as primary and God as secondary, then the whole purpose of religion has been stood on its head.

That is the basic error of Spiritualism as a religion. Not only does it make the psychic faculty central to its whole system of beliefs, it majors almost exclusively on one single aspect of the psychic faculty, the aspect which deals with the alleged communication between psychic sensitives and discarnate souls. Spiritualism as a religion is all about me and my survival, or my departed loved ones and their survival, and God is brought in (if he is brought in at all) simply as a guarantor of that survival. That kind of attitude cannot be the basis of a complete religious system because it only concerns itself with one narrow aspect of the whole panoply of individual and community life.

When, in 1937, Archbishop Lang set up a Committee under Francis Underhill to 'investigate the subject of communications with discarnate spirits and the claims of Spiritualism in relation to

Christian parapsychology

the Christian faith', the Chairman asked his cousin Evelyn Underhill, the noted writer and spiritual guide, to serve on it. Though at first she accepted, she resigned from the Committee after only one meeting, because she was so appalled at the unspiritual nature of so much into which she was being asked to enquire. In her letter of resignation, she said that reading the introductory material which had been circulated to the members of the Committee made her

> struck once more with the utterly sub-Christian, anthropocentric, hopelessly unsupernatural character of the Spiritualist outlook. It is all about man, his survival, prospects, etc., hardly at all about God, and really represents *au fond* the nineteenth-century naturalistic attitude with a little superstition stirred in. There is nothing here about the specifically religious attitude of adoration and trust. The whole outlook is utilitarian. Not the glory of God but our own consolation, future well-being, etc., is in the foreground. Personal survival is made a primary issue, a 'reason' for faith. And we are encouraged to bolster up our beliefs by experimental proofs that it is true; whereas surely for *religion* survival only matters in so far as it is part of the Will of God.

Strong words, but they needed to be said.

Spiritualists can become obsessive about their beliefs (so can some Christians). Many of them taunt Christians because they hold their beliefs as a matter of unsupported faith whilst Spiritualists have 'proof' of what they assert. But the Christian faith has different kinds of support, and the 'proofs' of Spiritualism are only inferences from ambiguous data.

There are, of course, almost as many different varieties of Spiritualism as there are of Christianity. Some Spiritualists are quite unashamedly humanistic and believe only in the permanent survival of discarnate human beings in a future life or a series of future lives from which the idea of God has been totally excluded. The Spiritualists' National Union is honest enough to deny accreditation of new chapels into its organisation unless they remove all Christian symbols from their meeting rooms. Most Spiritualists believe in some sort of cosmic force or power which may reveal itself to human beings in moments of numinous ecstasy and which acts as a guarantor of human survival. Others sing hymns from a bowdlerised Christian book, and some Spiritualists believe that Jesus of Nazareth was one of the greatest (or even the greatest) psychic medium of all time. After all, did he not bring Moses and Elijah back from the dead in quasi-physical form, and carry on a conversation with them on the Mount of the Transfiguration?

None of these Spiritualist organisations has a large membership. Their heyday was in the first half of the twentieth century, in the shadow of the mass bereavements caused by the carnage of the First World War. Today, we live in an age of believing rather than belonging. Very few people nowadays wish to be associated with any organisation or religion which requires regular attendance or worship. Their beliefs, they say, are their own private concern, and they prefer to follow their own do-it-yourself, pick-and-mix religion rather than have any of their beliefs prescribed for them by organised bodies.

It is when faced by a bereavement that many people need help. They would like to be persuaded that their departed loved ones are still alive in another set of dimensions, and that they remain within that same bond of love which supported them during their earthly lives. For many, that help can be given by their religious faith, and through the pastoral counsel they receive from the clergy or Christian friends. Others may be unpersuaded by this, and require some more concrete proof that death is not the end, and that there is hope of an eventual reunion. But this is not the same as joining a Spiritualist congregation and remaining a member of it. A single sitting with a medium may provide sufficient reassurance for them to be able to continue their lives by completing the process of mourning.

Even such a limited course of action has its dangers, and ought not to be enterprised without careful Christian counsel. It is all too easy to become stuck at a particular point in the psychology of bereavement, the point at which the death of the loved one is denied against all the evidence, a point through which many bereaved people have to pass if they are to build up their lives again after the trauma of losing someone whom they so dearly loved.

Bereavement counsellors know that clients who get held up at any one point of the bereavement process need to be helped through it, and that it can be psychologically harmful to remain at an inappropriate point of that painful journey. To hold on to the hope of receiving continuing messages from the loved one who has gone before us is to deny the possibility of further progress in the passage through bereavement to acceptance of the new situation, and may keep a mourner permanently in a kind of fantasy life. This can happen to anyone who joins a Spiritualist organisation, as well as to a person who has come to rely on the comfort of making regular visits to a psychic sensitive. For all we know, this activity may also hinder the post-mortem progress of the departed soul, who can, by our own selfishness, be held back in an earth-directed environment instead of progressing further in the exploration of the life of the world to come.

What is true psychologically is also true spiritually. Excessive reliance on a particular reading of the parapsychological data can hold a person back at an infantile point in the spiritual life, and render them unable to move on to a more mature kind of faith. Psychical research may reveal some unusual and fascinating things about human abilities, but if they are to be responsibly used, these abilities have to be exercised only to the glory of God and not simply to satisfy human curiosity. The psychical may be able to illuminate various aspects of the spiritual in a number of ways, but it should never be allowed to take its place. The archetypal human sin is to make human desires determinative, and the glory of God secondary. Human beings in their natural state are eccentric, in the sense that they look for their centre in themselves, whereas the true centre should be God, his purpose and his will. Only a radical reversal of this tendency, by which individuals find their true meaning, not in their own self, but in God, will cure this spiritually fatal condition. It is so easy to fix on the fascination of psychic phenomena in such a way that they feed our sinful self-centredness instead of opening to us the glories of God whose creation is so much more wonderful than we can conceive.

There are other dangers. Unfortunately, some mediums are mistaken about the extent of their powers, or even (in some sad cases) completely fraudulent. The practice can attract the psychically or psychologically unstable. The genuine medium is open to all sorts of stray psychic influences, not all of which are benevolent. The initiative may come from beings who are not within the Communion of Saints, but who have a need to feed upon the psychic powers of humans whom they will then use to their own ends. The gift of psychic sensitivity needs to be exercised to the glory of God and in his service, and the sensitive needs to be surrounded by Christian prayer and counsel at all times, as a protection against the influx of ill-intentioned discarnate entities.

Discernment and discrimination are always vital. 'My dear friends' warns the First Letter of John in the New Testament,

> Do not trust every spirit, but test the spirits, to see whether they are from God; for there are many false prophets about in the world. The way to recognise the Spirit of God is this: every spirit which acknowledges that Jesus Christ has come in the flesh is from God, and no spirit is from God which does not acknowledge Jesus (1 John 4.1-3).

#

With all these warnings, who would want to exercise such a faculty? The fact is, that for those who have it, it is not a matter of choice. Some people are naturally psychic, as others are naturally musically- or mathematically-inclined. They have been given a particular talent by God, and it is for them to learn to exercise this talent to his glory and the good of other people. Any talent has its dangers as well as its opportunities. The dangers are greatest when they are unperceived, which is why there is such a body as the Churches' Fellowship for Psychical and Spiritual Studies, which can help guide psychically sensitive Christians through the possible snares.

Some people find that they are unable to cope with their psychic sensitivity, and that it runs away with them and makes them unable to operate properly in the physical world. For them it may be necessary to eschew the practice of their sensitivity. This is not to say that sensitivity is always suspect, only that for some people it is not possible to exercise it in moderation. To give an analogy, alcohol is a gift of God which can add enormously to human well-being, relaxation, and sociability, but some people are incapable of its responsible use and the only way out is by total abstinence. The fact that some people have to be tee-totallers does not make alcohol evil. The fact that some people have to avoid the exercise of their psychic sensitivity does not mean that others should be forbidden to use this particular gift to help other people.

Indeed, some of the people they help in this particular way may be human beings who have departed this life and lost their way in the life of the world to come. Just as evangelists are able to show their converts the way to salvation, so Christian 'rescue circles' exist in order that psychically sensitive people may help lost discarnate souls find their way to Jesus. There can be no greater work than to open people's eyes to the glories that God has in store for us all.

The late Chancellor Garth Moore, QC, a very distinguished lawyer and a priest of the Church of England, former President of the Churches' Fellowship, believed that 'sight should never be lost of the fact that psychic awareness (of which mediumship is but a facet) is a very great gift from God, like any of the recognised five senses'. It can therefore be legitimately exercised, so long as this is done in a responsible and Christian manner.

The Christian churches have begun the process. As long ago as 1922, the General Assembly of the Church of Scotland received the report of a Committee which expressed the hope that Christians who had been vouchsafed special psychic manifestations 'should be encouraged to share in the life of the Church rather than to withdraw themselves from its communion'. In 1976, the United Presbyterian Church of the USA set up a Task Force on Occult and Psychic Activities. It presented guidelines for pastors

Psychical and Spiritual

and sessions, and asked them to discriminate between such practices as honoured God and witnessed to him, and such practices as did not do so. They are worth reproducing here as an example of the questions Christians need to ask about the exercise of psychic sensitivity.

1. Does the psychic event or phenomenon lead us as total persons - heart, soul and mind - to love the Lord our God, putting no other gods before him, and to love our neighbors as ourselves?

2. Does it witness to the sovereignty of God as the ultimate source of possibility, power and resources; or is it ego-centric and manipulative, concerned primarily with private power?

3. Does it honor God's chosen means of self-revelation: his Son, his Word, and his Spirit?

4. Does it honor God's creation, both nature and humanity, in terms of fostering wholeness, reconciliation, and a posture of self-sacrificial servanthood rather than exploitation in both personal and societal terms? Is the 'unlovable' and the enemy given at least equal status within this redemptive framework? Is human need, bodily as well as spiritual, an item of concern and action?

5. Is it open to the infinite variety of God's work in the world, with humble recognition that 'His ways are not our ways', leaving room for unknowns, for natural and general revelation, for fellowship with any and all human beings, whatever their faith, ethnicity or theology, providing they do not despoil the human or seek to subvert love and community?

6. Does it produce in the long run, the 'fruits of the Spirit': love, joy, peace, patience, kindness, goodness, faithfulness, gentleness and self-control?

7. Does it promote humility, a recognition that we do not yet see God 'face to face', but only 'through a glass darkly', that much is yet incomprehensible or unknown, that we yet have much to learn and perhaps to relearn about his ways?

Those are searching questions, and much that is vaunted as of importance in the psychic world would not survive examination in the light of them. But they need to be asked, and the fact that a

Christian church has produced them as criteria for the assessment of this body of human experience shows that the task of Christian discrimination is well under way.

#

Two particular areas where Christian practice and parapsychology could well overlap are prayer and healing.

Do our prayers work? If so, do we know *how* or *why* they work? Archbishop Temple (1881-1944) used to claim that when he said his prayers, coincidences happened, but that when he neglected to say them the coincidences stopped. If answers to prayer are more than coincidental, can they be explained purely parapsychologically? Could it, for example, be that if we direct our thoughts towards the welfare of another person, they can act on that person by some kind of psycho-kinesis and do them good? Or perhaps the person who is prayed for can be telepathically aware (consciously or unconsciously) of the beneficent thoughts which are being pointed in their direction? If so, answers to prayer may be the work of God in that God is responsible for the laws of parapsychology as he is responsible for all other scientific laws; but they are, as one might say, God's impersonal work.

That is not how Christians understand prayer. For them, prayer is above all else a means of consciously putting oneself in the presence of God, of conversing with him, and of seeking to bring the people for whom one is praying into his presence, so that he may bring them into alignment with his purposes. Any suggestion that prayer was akin to putting a coin in the slot-machine and getting the bar of chocolate out would be anathema to anyone who took Christian prayer seriously.

If it seems to us that God is taking no notice of our prayers, it may be that perhaps he has other ideas than we have. When we say our prayers, we must guard against the temptation to tell God what we think it would be best for him to do. He is not going to let his creation dictate to him, though we believe he always has its best interests in mind.

The better prayers are those which place the object of our intercessions in God's presence and ask that the obstacles to his will might be overcome and that he would do what he knows to be best. Anything more specific than that runs the danger of being presumptuous.

In any case, it is not easy to formulate any experiment or statistical analysis to see whether the prayers we offer for our loved ones, or for those whose welfare concerns us, have made any appreciable difference to them. It has often been pointed out that though the prayer 'God save the Queen' (or King) has been offered daily throughout the kingdom for centuries, our own monarchs have been no more healthy or long-lived than the world leaders of non-Christian nations. Perhaps this is because our own prayers are counter-weighted by the prayers of our enemies, who wish to confound our politics and frustrate our knavish tricks? Or perhaps it is because, when we pray for the Royal Family, our prayers are formal and distant and have no genuine intent; they come from the tongue, not the heart, and do not engage us emotionally?

About the only area in which it is possible to calculate the effectiveness of prayer is when it is a prayer for healing.

We believe that health of body and mind is God's will for all his creatures, and we know that sickness and disease are endemic in the world we live in. Is it possible to do anything paranormally to forward God's purposes in this respect?

There are at least three kinds of paranormal or spiritual healing. *Faith-healing* is brought about by suggestion, hypnotic or otherwise, operating through the mind or psyche of the patient. It seems as though it can be exercised either directly by the healer to whom the patient comes for treatment; or it may be operated at a distance by some telepathic or quasi-telepathic means. When it is successful, it has enabled the patient's mind to interact with their body (by some psychosomatic means) so that the natural processes of healing are stimulated or the body's immune responses are heightened. The patient may even be entirely unaware that this particular form of healing has been effected, because the telepathic contact has been made at a subconscious level.

This form of paranormal healing shades off into the next, which is *psychic healing*. Here, the stimulus seems to travel body-to-body rather than through the mind. In the seventeenth century, the Stuart monarchs used to cure scrofula by applying the royal touch to the patient. Whether we should regard that as an example of psycho-somatic relief by faith healing or as a purely physiological case of psychic healing is probably no more than a matter of nomenclature. There have, however, been experiments on mice and plants, and even on bacteria, which have shown that some healers are able, by laying their hands on the cage or pot or dish, to speed up the healing of wounds or to cause plants to grow or organisms to multiply much faster than the control samples. It seems that some people have powers of healing, or powers of encouraging growth, which are psychic in nature.

And, thirdly, there is *miraculous healing* which has been known from time immemorial and which is believed to involve divine intervention. The cures at Lourdes may be among them, but it should be noted that they are infrequent (only twenty-two cases were authenticated by the Roman Catholic authorities there in the twenty-five years between 1946 and 1972) and impossible to foretell. That is not surprising if they are truly divinely caused, for God is not likely to limit himself to our timing or to our expectations.

Most Christians, however, are not gifted with healing powers, but many of them regularly engage in prayers for healing. Is there any evidence that their prayers are of any use?

There is, and experiments are still being carried on in an attempt to collect such evidence. A study by Dr Randolph Byrd in 1988 showed that, of four hundred patients in a coronary care unit, the two hundred who received intercessory prayer had a less complicated hospital course and required fewer medications and procedures than the two hundred who belonged to the control group and were not prayed for in the same way. More recently, Dr William Harris carried out an investigation which involved 990 patients in the Mid America Heart Institute. Half of them were prayed for, over a period of a month, by a team of seventy-five intercessors. They fared better than the control group.

The most recent survey of this kind was described by Professor Russell Stannard in the *Christian Parapsychologist* for September 2000. As a Trustee of the Templeton Foundation, an American charitable organisation supporting understanding between scientific and religious thought and practice, Dr Stannard has been studying a project led by Dr Herbert Benson of Boston. Patients admitted to any one of five US hospitals because they were suffering from heart disease and needed bypass surgery were asked whether they agreed to take part in the experiment. The 1200 patients who agreed to take part were assigned to one of two groups, without knowing to which they were to belong, and without the medical staff who tended them knowing this, either. The first were prayed for by teams of intercessors drawn from a variety of religious denominations who were told the Christian names of the patients and broad details of their medical condition, but nothing else about them. The second group were not prayed for in this way, though it would be surprising if their relatives and friends were not saying prayers for them. But then, the first group would also have the benefit of the 'normal' prayers of their supporters as well as the 'special' prayers of the intercessory teams. Over three years, their case histories are being followed up to see if there are significant differences between the two groups. In addition, there is a third group of 600 patients who are being prayed for and who *know* they are being prayed for, so the researchers can see whether there is any advantage in knowing that one is the subject of prayer. The final analysis should be available soon, but too late to be reported here.

If the scientific and medical worlds agree that it is experimentally proven that prayer is an important agency in the healing process, there could be some odd by-products. Our politicians might judge that since nuns are less expensive than cardiac surgeons, they should save on the costs of the NHS by employing more people to pray and fewer to perform operations. And what about the possibilities of litigation for malpractice? If prayer works, could non-praying doctors be sued for neglect? Ought doctors to seek consent from their patients before praying, just as they have to do before operating? Could an atheist sue a doctor for praying for him without consent? The mind begins to boggle at the possibilities.

Some Christians are uneasy about the whole business of carrying out tests or experiments to see whether prayer is effective. In part this is because they think that a negative result will discourage people from praying and a positive one will mean that people will be tempted only to pray to God for material benefits rather than spiritual health. In part there is the fear of being guilty of 'putting God to the test', a sin which is roundly condemned by the Bible on several occasions (see, for example, Deuteronomy 6.16, quoted by Jesus himself at Matthew 4.7).

We can deal with that last question first. None of these procedures will identify cases in which prayer has influenced the outcome of any particular person's illness. The most they can do is to show that there is a statistical link between prayer and the restoration of bodily health. Some of the people who have been prayed for, will get better. Some will not. Exactly the same will be true of the people who have not been prayed for. No-one could ever know which of the people who recovered, would have failed to do so had they not been prayed for. That is a secret which God will keep for ever. We are not trying to discover a way of curing people by prayer; we are simply trying to show that prayer is one weapon in the Christian healer's armamentarium. The writer of Ecclesiasticus in the Apocrypha knew that medical care and prayer were both essential for a full cure :

> My son, in time of illness do not be remiss,
> but pray to the Lord and he will heal you. ...
> And the doctor should be called;
> keep him by you, for you need him also (Ecclesiasticus 38. 9,12).

But if we were to prove the effectiveness of healing prayer, would it encourage people to ask for prayer for purely physical, unspiritual reasons? Probably, yes. But that is no different from what people do today. When they are ill they pray for a cure. Christians know that cure and healing are not the same thing, and that God's will may be shown in more than one outcome of an illness. What is most important is a person's relation with God, and we should be praying that that will be deepened and strengthened by whatever trials and tribulations a person has to pass through. Yet we believe that health of body is as much God's ultimate will as health of soul, and that even an atheistic physician is doing God's work as he works to restore a person's body to proper functioning.

The best thing is to pray that God's will may be as perfectly operative as is possible in a world where the forces of sin, evil, and ill-health are at work. We must hope, as we pray for our loved ones, that that will mean that they will return to normal functioning; but we must be prepared for other outcomes, and for God's will to be worked out through them in other ways than through that particular scenario we had in mind when we offered our prayers for them.

Certainly, prayer is never a waste of time. Of course God could do his will without our prayerful co-operation, but somehow, he seems to want to honour us by using us as co-operative workers with him. He has set in our minds an urge to pray, and he would not mock us by making it a useless urge.

#

Life is not easy for people who have psychic sensitivity, especially for Christians who possess this particular ability in more than an average degree.

Some of them will have known about it from childhood, but they will have learnt very early on in life that most adults did not understand that what they were seeing or feeling was real. They would have been told not to have so vivid an imagination, so they would soon have learned that there were aspects of their life about which it was better not to tell anybody else. They may have lived their whole life keeping quiet about something which was an intimate part of themselves and yet which, so they felt, would be sadly misunderstood by even their closest friends.

Others will have become aware of their psychic potentialities later on in life. Perhaps they had a dream which became true, or a premonition that something was about to happen; or they suddenly thought about a friend who had not come into their mind for ages, and when they rang them up, they found that something had happened to them and they could be of help in an emergency. Or they saw something in their mind's eye and then read about it in the news a few days later. At first, there was nothing particularly special about such dreams or premonitions. It was not that they were particularly vivid, or that they felt there was something about them which marked them out from the every-day, run-of-the-mill, thoughts which flitted through their consciousness. Only later, and for some people more than others, could they detect a certain frisson about particular experiences, so that they were able to tell in advance that certain dreams were 'true' ones, or certain intuitions had a special meaning. But often, there is no such frisson, and it is only subsequent events which make a person suddenly exclaim, 'I was dreaming about this thing a couple of nights ago!'

It can be very worrying, especially if it begins to happen at all frequently. What is a person supposed to do if they discover they seem to have paranormal powers and that they are beginning to receive privileged information, either about the future or about what is happening to other people in the present? The dilemma is particularly acute if they are Christians, and their pastor, or friends in their congregation, are strongly affected by anti-paranormal bias. Will they be ridiculed if they start talking about the things that are happening to them? Can they own up to having such experiences? Are things like this, healthy? Are they from God? Or are they, perhaps, delusions from God's enemy?

Anybody who has read thus far should realise that there is nothing intrinsically evil or unhealthy about knowledge acquired paranormally. Nor is it as unusual as many people think. Of course it needs to be assessed critically. Some apparent premonitions are simply coincidences with no inner significance. Some people who imagine themselves to be psychically gifted may in fact be psychologically unbalanced. Anyone who believes that they may have these strange and occasional powers ought to be able to find friends and guides who can ensure that they do not go spiritually or psychologically off the rails. That, of course, is not easy, because of the conspiracy of silence and misunderstanding that is still so rife. One of the important functions of the Churches' Fellowship for Psychical and Spiritual Studies is to act as a 'safe house' for people who wish to assess their psychic experiences in a critical but friendly atmosphere, and who need to be in touch with someone who can act as a spiritual guide in these areas. All too often, people with psychic sensitivity look to a psychic teacher who can help them develop their gift, when what they really need is a spiritual guide to help them come to terms with it and use it to God's glory and their own well-being. The Churches' Fellowship does not exist in order to train Christians in psychic technique. It exists in order to help Christian psychics seek and do God's will.

The question still arises, What should be done about paranormally acquired information, either about the present or the future? Should it be encouraged, or should it be avoided?

Avoidance is not easy. If a person is psychically sensitive, that is part of their nature. These moments happen, and there is nothing easy or immediate that can be done to stop them. There are some people who find the whole experience of psychic sensitivity so un-nerving, so unsettling, so unwelcome, that they feel they are not able to cope with possession of this particular talent. They may be right. In that case, they can pray that God may take this unwanted gift away from them, and he may grant them their request. But they will from then on, live a truncated life, which, at least, is far from ideal. As we have already said, there may be people for whom that is the case, just as there are people who have to abjure alcohol because they cannot otherwise control their use of it. But where the gift of sensitivity is concerned, it is better to learn control than to repress what can be an enriching part of total life.

At the other extreme are people who wish to develop their psychic powers, and there are many organisations which will enrol people on courses for this purpose. They often claim to be able to train their pupils to be more effective clairvoyants or fortune-tellers or mediums, sometimes promising a profitable professional career in this field. On the whole, they are to be avoided. Psychic intuition is healthier if it is exercised spontaneously, as God gives, rather than relied upon to work to order.

When psychic intuitions arise, there are several ways of dealing with them. The possibility must always be held in mind that they are inaccurate. Even if they are accompanied by the tell-tale signs which the person experiencing them has come to recognise as indicating that they are genuine, they should be treated with caution. If you have the intuition that something dreadful has happened to a close friend, you should ring to enquire of them in a completely neutral way. It would only cause unnecessary alarm if you rang to say that you had an intuition that something untoward had happened.

What, though, if you feel that something untoward has not yet happened, but is being foretold through you? If it is a very specific intuition, for example that there will be a road accident involving that person the next time he goes to work, you may wish to advise him to use a different route for the next few days.

Many premonitions are less specific than this. Many of them seem at the time to be rather general in their import, and to involve people we never knew, or occasions which are nothing whatever to do with us; and then, later on, we realise that they were advance glimpses of things about which we subsequently read in the newspapers or saw on the television. There have been reports of people who believe that they had precognitions of the Tianamen Square massacre, or of the atrocities in New York and Washington on 11 September 2001. Many people claim to have foretold particular airline accidents. What can people do if they have premonitions like this? There is encouraging research, to which we alluded on page 37 above, which suggests that precognitions are only foreshadowings of possibilities, not of certainties, and that the only precognitions which have proved to be true are ones where the person who has had them has not tried to avert them, or has had no possible way of preventing them from happening. We only precognise what we cannot affect. So we should not feel guilty of causing harm by neglect if we receive a premonition and do nothing to warn the person about whom it is made.

That will not prevent us from feeling a concern for the person or the occasion we seem to be foreseeing. But Christians will know that one of the best things to do about concerns where we are powerless to affect their outcome is to treat that concern as an invitation to prayer. Prayer, as we have said, is not an attempt to twist God's arm. It is an activity which aims to put the person or the occasion in the hands of God, confident that what will happen will be for the best, or that, if disaster strikes, some good may come out of it, or its victims will be strengthened to bear it. Particularly if the premonition is less specific than the ones we have just mentioned, and it would be irresponsible to frighten our friends by saying that we have (for instance) foreseen an accident or an illness or a death at an unspecified time in the future, the only sensible Christian course of action is to keep that person regularly in our prayers, and trust God to use for his purposes whatever the future may bring. Perhaps, who knows?, our very prayers will be instrumental in averting the threatened disaster. Precognition is always a foretaste of possibilities, not of certainties. We are not puppets in the hands of fate, or automata set to go along predetermined lines. We are creatures of God endued with the freewill which enables us to mould our futures. There is nothing about the paranormal which can take away the fact that humans are responsible spiritual beings. Parapsychology, for a Christian, involves spirituality.

#

Why have I tried for so many years to be a Christian parapsychologist? It is not because I am particularly psychic in myself. At one time I believed myself to be completely devoid of that particular talent, but Dr Martin Israel explained to me that everybody was psychic in their own particular way and that it was the psychic faculty, for instance, which enabled a speaker to tell whether or not he was connecting with his audience (or a preacher with his congregation).

As I explained in the opening chapter of this book, my interest in the paranormal began as an intellectual search. I then became aware that psychics had a bad press, particularly amongst Chrisians, and my interests moved on, towards doing my best to ensure that their abilities got fair treatment. But it was only when I began to be associated with the Churches' Fellowship for Psychical and Spiritual Studies that I met so many fine, sincere, and intelligent Christians whose psychic gifts were devoted in Gods service, and I realised there was a task to be done in commending their insights to the wider Church.

When the Fellowship was founded, in the early 1950s, it spent much of its energy on the questions of survival and mediumship. Those questions are still with it, but its members in this present generation are far less excited by them, and certainly would not regard them as the most important issues facing Christians with psychic sensitivity. As Christian Aid used to say in its advertisements, we believe in life before death as well as life after death.

The Christian life is about far more than trying to prove that we will continue after the death of our bodies. That is one reason why, in its second decade, the Fellowship added the words 'and Spiritual' to its title. We are far more interested in the spiritual life than in psychic phenomena. That is why I have, so far, given absolutely no specific details about what we might expect after death; I have only discussed general possibilities, such as the choice between reincarnation onto this earth and survival into another kind of life in non-physical surroundings. Psychic sensitives can tell us a great deal about what we might expect and what our next life might be like; but nobody knows how far they are giving us an accurate description of the world of the life to come. For all we know, their interpretation of the material which they receive through their psychic sense may be hopelessly distorted and refracted through the lens of their own preconceptions, beliefs, and hopes. I prefer to put my trust in God, and to expect that he will have surprises in store for us - and those of us who were most certain about the exact details of what was going to happen to us are likely to be the most surprised!

If there is nothing more to our continued existence than the kind of activities about which so many psychic mediums tell their clients, then after death we might well have saved our lives but lost our souls - we might have become what the eighteenth-century hymn-writer Isaac Watts called 'hopeless immortals'. Survival of death might then be no more than an everlasting life sentence.

We do not want simply to keep on keeping on, with nothing to stave off our boredom but the prospect of an eternity of suburban tea-parties. We want life of a quality which makes it a joy to be alive. Christians believe that that kind of life is a special gift from God which he is longing to bestow on those who wish to find their life in him. It is a life which can begin here on this earth, but its fullness is reserved for the life of God's world to come. It is a life which we enter, not by surviving death, but by being resurrected into God's eternity. Christians hope that their lives will be lives marked by a growth in love - love *felt*, but also, essentially, love shown in practical expression towards God and their fellows. This kind of growth has nothing whatever to do with psychic gifts and everything to do with spiritual awareness.

Religion was once defined as 'that which a man does with his own solitariness'. That is no description of Christianity. The life of resurrection into God's eternity is essentially life in a community, known as the Body of Christ. That body is not a constricting straitjacket, but a body of support for a pilgrim people, who know that Christian truth is so marvellous that fresh avenues of discovery lie at every turn of the Way. Many members of the Churches' Fellowship are agnostic about details of the Christian creeds, and find it impossible to assent *ex animo* to every article in them. This does not mean that they are proponents of an *à la carte* or pick-and-mix religion. It means they are Christian explorers, who find the fullness of truth quite overwhelming and have to discover as much of it as they can take, a little at a time. They see the Church with its many imperfections, with so many teachings which they find hard to accept. But they find so many facets of truth within it, so many aspects of reality to which their innermost being resonates, that they cannot bear to break with it.

They are like the disciples, as described at the end of the sixth chapter of St John's Gospel. Jesus had been teaching them so many things which they found hard to take, and therefore many of the disciples left him at that stage. But when Jesus asked the Twelve whether they too wanted to leave him, Peter answered for them all by saying, 'Lord, to whom shall we go? Your words are words of eternal life' (John 6.66). Similarly, there are plenty of people who have their difficulties with Christian doctrines, but the alternative is too grim for them to contemplate. Jesus has the words of eternal life, and they intend to stick with him.

As Herbert Butterfield wrote more than half a century ago, at the end of his magisterial book *Christianity and History*, 'Hold to Christ, and for the rest be totally uncommitted'. We believe that if we hold to Christ, he will hold to us, whatever the imperfections in our understanding of God and his relations with us.

We are assured that God has prepared things for his elect which are beyond our understanding. That is certainly true if we limit that understanding to the kinds of logical thought which characterise our left hemispheres, but in their moments of ecstasy the saints and mystics (and, yes, many 'ordinary' Christians too, whether or not they have been blessed with any exceptional psychic talent) have caught a glimpse of what those ineffable promises might be like. In those moments, our perceptions go beyond intellectual notions into a more immediate apprehension of God. Then the Christian says, 'I no longer *believe*; I *know*'. God has become self-evident and beyond contradiction.

I have asked that, at my funeral, the congregation should sing the hymn 'The duteous day now closeth'. Two of its verses go:

>Now all the heavenly splendour
>Breaks forth in starlight tender
>   From myriad worlds unknown;
>And man, the marvel seeing,
>Forgets his selfish being,
>   For joy of beauty not his own.

Psychical and Spiritual

> His care he drowneth yonder,
> Lost in the abyss of wonder;
> To heaven his soul doth steal :
> This life he disesteemeth,
> The day it is that dreameth,
> That doth from truth his vision seal.

Because glimpses like that come to us through the right hemisphere of our brains, they are, quite literally, unspeakable. They are usually termed 'mystical', which means that they involve a unity between the psychical and the spiritual in which we can begin to grasp at last the full truth behind the statement that the chief end of man is to glorify God and enjoy him for ever.

To that glory and enjoyment may he bring us all!

Index

Angels 71ff
Augustinianism 91
Aura 30, 38, 51
Automatic writing 112

Bereavement visions 41, 108, 131
Body 23ff, 27
Boggle threshold 19, 60
Brain function 41, 98

CFPSS 17, 47, 88, 142, 145
Chain of being 87f
Christian Parapsychologist 17
Cold reading 41
Consciousness 45, 96
Crisis apparition 40, 108

Death 95, 120
Deathbed visions 109, 110
Demons 88ff
Dionysius 83f
Discernment 132, 134
Dispensationalism 62
Divination 52, 65
Division of consciousness 118
Dowsing 38

Electromagnetic fields 33
Exorcism 54, 93

Extra-sensory perception 48

Faith and evidence 18
Fear 122
Flesh 28
Fraud 56, 111

Ganzfeld 10
Group Soul 118

Healing 39, 54, 136ff
Hypnotism 101

Irenaeus 91

Levitical prohibitions 65ff, 124

Mediumship 41, 52, 66f, 111, 130, 133, 145
Memes 97f
Meta-analysis 11
Mind and matter 44f
Miracles 47, 50, 58

Near-death experience 24, 51, 110
Neurophysiology 42, 44

Occult 31
Ouija 41, 94
Out-of-body experience 24

Past life recall 101ff
Place memories 38, 90
Planchette 41
Plato 24
Poltergeist 5, 19, 93
Possession 92
Prayer 135, 144
Premonitions 36, 49, 143
Presbyterian criteria 134
Projection 41
Proof 129
Psychokinesis 39, 49

Quantum mechanics 46, 64

Reincarnation 98ff, 115
Remote viewing 37
Resurrection 4, 5, 28, 62, 64, 69, 120

Satan 54, 91
Scientism 44, 46, 60
Scole group 39
Sensitivity 134, 140
Society for Psychical Research 13, 37

Socrates 23
Soul 23-30, 118
Space 85
Spirit 29, 118
Spiritualism 70, 128
Statistical analysis 5
Survival 107ff, 145ff
Swedenborg 84, 86, 127

Telepathy 9, 35, 48, 57
Teleportation 50
Trance 53
Transfiguration 39, 51

UFOs 51

Visions 52f, 72
Voices 53

Witch of En-Dor 52, 67, 127

Xenoglossy 53

The Churches' Fellowship
for Psychical and Spiritual Studies

The CFPSS exists to promote the study and the integration of psychical and spiritual experience within a Christian context. Founded in 1953, it continues to serve churches and individuals with many and varied backgrounds, experiences and needs. Its patrons include the Archbishop of York and the Bishop of London, as well as prominent Christians from other major denominations.

Many people have come to value the guidance of the Fellowship when they have experienced spontaneous gifts of the Spirit, the pain of bereavement or simply a call to deeper spiritual understanding. The Fellowship offers a safe meeting place where members and enquirers may share and explore these experiences, both psychical and spiritual, in an open atmosphere of love and acceptance. Fellowship members can help to bring an enriching wisdom and a depth of vision and understanding to such experiences.

The CFPSS operates at a local, regional and national level, providing fellowship and opportunities to share and study at residential and one-day conferences, and at local group and branch meetings. It also publishes two journals, *The Christian Parapsychologist* and *The Quarterly Review*, sent free to all members.

There are two categories of membership: full and associate. Those eligible for full membership must be members of a Christian church and/or must acknowledge Jesus Christ as Lord and Saviour of the world. A reference is required from either a minister of a Christian church or a full member of the Fellowship.

Associate membership is open to all without the need for reference, but such members are not eligible to hold office or to vote.

There is a library at Head Office for the use of all members, operated on a postal basis, with outward postage paid by the Fellowship. A full catalogue is available.

Books, booklets, audio and video tapes are available for borrowing or purchase, and a series of study notes on a variety of subjects has been prepared for individual or group use. Full details are available from the General Secretary, at the address below.

CFPSS,
The Rural Workshop, South Road, North Somercotes
Louth, Lincolnshire LN11 7PT
Telephone and fax : 01507 358845
e-mail : gensec@cfpss.freeserve.co.uk